COMBAT ARMS

MODERN

SUBMARINES

DAVID MILLER

a Salamander book

Published by Salamander Books Limited
LONDON • NEW YORK

A Salamander Book

Published by
Salamander Books Ltd.,
52 Bedford Row,
London WC1R 4LR,
United Kingdom.

©Salamander Books Ltd. 1989

ISBN 0 86101 450 2

Distributed in the United Kingdom by
Hodder & Stoughton Services
PO Box 6, Mill Road
Dunton Green, Sevenoaks,
Kent TN13 2XX.

All correspondence concerning the content of
this volume should be addressed to the publisher.

Credits

Editor: Graham Smith.
Designed by: The Maltings Partnership, ©Salamander
Books Ltd.
Colour artwork: ©Salamander Books Ltd.
Filmset by The Old Mill, London.
Colour reproduction: Planographic Studios Ltd.
Printed in Belgium by: Proost International
Book Production, Turnhout.

The Author

David Miller is a serving officer in the British Army and his
career has included service in the Royal Corps of Signals,
several staff posts and command of a Regiment in the UK. He
has contributed to many military books and technical articles
on defence affairs, including Salamander's Illustrated Guides to
''Modern Submarines'' and ''Modern Subhunters''. He is the
co-author of the Salamander encyclopedias ''Modern Naval
Combat'' and ''Modern Submarine Warfare'', and has
contributed to ''The Vietnam War'', ''The Balance of Military
Power'' and ''The Intelligence War''.

Contents

THERE IS A quiet and largely unseen maritime revolution in progress as submarines become the most important element in naval warfare. The number of submarines and of navies with a submarine arm grow every year and technology transfer is enabling more nations to produce these sophisticated war machines. Up to 1987 there were five navies (the British, French, American, Soviet and the People's Republic of China) operating nuclear-powered submarine fleets, but in 1988 these were joined by India. Other nations, too, are known to be planning to operate nuclear-powered submarines of their own, including Canada, Brazil and Argentina. Further, there are indications of a technological breakthrough which could enable non-nuclear submarines to operate for protracted periods without returning to the surface, thus overcoming the major remaining problem for this type.

Until the mid-1960s the primary role of submarines was to attack hostile surface warships and merchant ships. This role still exists, but submarine-launched ballistic and cruise missiles have brought a further strategic role, that of striking directly at targets in the enemy's homeland. The third role is that of attack against other submarines. While nuclear-powered attack submarines (SSNs) are most effective in this role, the diesel-electric submarine (SSK) still has a major role and many hundreds are operational with some 39 navies, employed in attack missions, in general "patrol" duties and in clandestine "special duties".

Design

The German Type XXI submarine of 1945 introduced a combination of streamlining, powerful electric motors and a snorkel, which created a true submarine warship. However, the long and narrow hulls proved unable to cope with the increased power and, under certain conditions, control could be lost; thus, USS *Nautilus* (SSN 571), the first nuclear-propelled submarine with a hull designed on these principles, could not exceed 23.3 knots underwater.

The 1950s saw two further revolutionary developments: nuclear propulsion and the "teardrop" hull. The latter was pioneered by the diesel-electric powered USS *Albacore*, which, with its teardrop hull (based on airship practice), cruciform tail empennage and single propeller, achieved sustained underwater speeds of 26 knots. Later, with contra-rotating propellers and silver-zinc batteries, she achieved an astonishing 33 knots. Not surprisingly, she set the general pattern for the majority of subsequent Western hull designs.

A submerged submarine must have neutral buoyancy, with the centre-of-gravity below the centre-of-buoyancy. The

Some nuclear-powered attack submarines in service

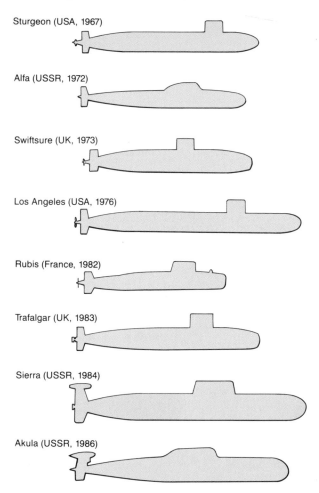

Sturgeon (USA, 1967)

Alfa (USSR, 1972)

Swiftsure (UK, 1973)

Los Angeles (USA, 1976)

Rubis (France, 1982)

Trafalgar (UK, 1983)

Sierra (USSR, 1984)

Akula (USSR, 1986)

distribution of weight within the submarine is crucial to its stability and the mass of items such as fuel, stores, weapons and provisions must be constantly taken into account. The compressibility of the hull is a further factor, since in a deep-diving submarine this could result in a loss of buoyancy of several tons at depth.

Diving depth is another consideration. Depth provides shelter, especially if the submarine can achieve sufficient depth to exploit the acoustic properties of the sea to thwart anti-submarine warfare (ASW) detection devices. Actual details are highly classified, but open-source figures give some indication of normal operating depths for comparative purposes. The Los Angeles SSN (United States) can reach over 1,500ft (450m), the Victor III SSN (USSR) 1,300ft (400m)

Some ballistic missile submarines in service

Lafayette (USA, 1963)

Yankee (USSR, 1967)

Resolution (UK, 1967)

Le Redoutable (France, 1971)

Ohio (USA, 1981)

Typhoon (USSR, 1981)

Xia (China, 1985)

Delta (USSR, 1985)

Above: Los Angeles class nuclear-powered submarine USS Birmingham (SSN-695) *surfaces in spectacular fashion. Nuclear propulsion has freed submarines from the need to surface regularly.*

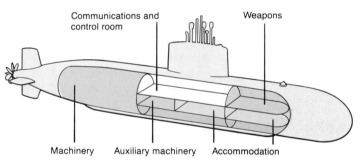

Communications and control room

Weapons

Machinery   Auxiliary machinery   Accommodation

Upholder class space allocation

Above: The use in Upholder of two watertight bulkheads dividing the pressure hull into three main compartments is unusual today, but contributes to the exceptional structural integrity of this class.

and the French Rubis SSN is capable of 980ft (300m).

Such depth performance is becoming more important as the ASW threat increases and is naturally leading to extensive research and development into materials. It also requires a much more detailed knowledge of the geography of the ocean floor, which is why there is such an increase in "oceanographic ships" in many navies.

Considerable research is being carried out into hydrodynamic efficiency. The total resistance (drag) of a submerged submarine has three elements: skin friction, form drag and appendage drag. Skin friction is proportional to the surface area of the hull; form drag is usually some 2 to 4 per cent of the total; while appendages (e.g. sonar domes) add drag, no matter how well designed.

A badly finished hull (e.g. with poorly designed flood openings) has considerable drag as well as being noisy. Special hull paints can reduce friction, as can releasing polymers around the hull. Reports suggest that Soviet submarines are coated with a compliant covering, which combines suction and boundary-layer pressure equalisation. Further development may lead to devices to modify shapes to match the boat's speed; e.g. changing the fin shape as speed increases. It is noticeable that the latest Soviet submarines have bulbous bows, similar to the front end of a whale, while their sails are smaller and less angular that those on Western submarines, appearing more akin to the streamlined fin of many fast-swimming marine animals.

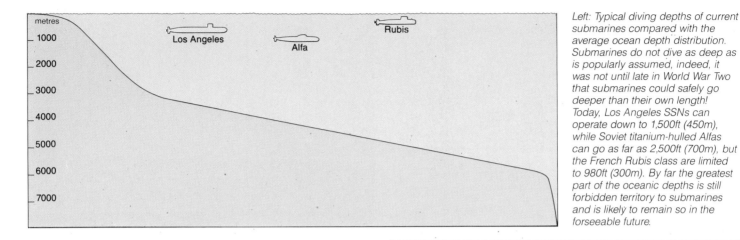

Left: Typical diving depths of current submarines compared with the average ocean depth distribution. Submarines do not dive as deep as is popularly assumed, indeed, it was not until late in World War Two that submarines could safely go deeper than their own length! Today, Los Angeles SSNs can operate down to 1,500ft (450m), while Soviet titanium-hulled Alfas can go as far as 2,500ft (700m), but the French Rubis class are limited to 980ft (300m). By far the greatest part of the oceanic depths is still forbidden territory to submarines and is likely to remain so in the forseeable future.

Sturgeon class antennas and masts

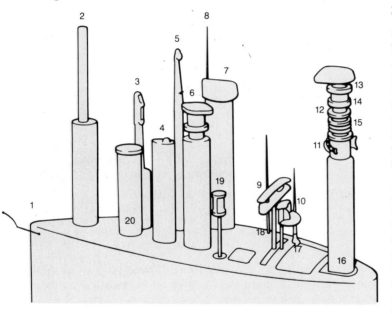

1	AS-1554/BRM(20) floating wire antenna	8 AT-497/BRC snorkel whip antenna
2	AS-1792/BRA-21 helical antenna	9 AS-164A/BPS-14 surface search radar antenna
3	Observation periscope	10 Masthead light
4	AS-1201/BPX IFF/UHF antenna	11 AS-994/BLR directional antenna
5	Attack periscope	12 AS-1584/BLR omni-directional antenna
6	AS-1907/BRD-6 direction-finding antenna	13 AS-1071A/BLR directional antenna
7	Snorkel induction mast	14 AS-1649/0 omni-

directional antenna
15 AS-962/BLR directional antenna
16 ECM/DF antenna mast
17 AT-774A/UR portable emergency whip antenna
18 AT-441/MRC portable emergency whip antenna
19 Identification beacon
20 AT-317F/BRR loop antenna

Construction

There are four main types of hull arrangement. Single-hull submarines have their main ballast tanks mounted either externally at each end of the pressure hull (e.g. US Navy Los Angeles-class SSN), or within the hull itself. Saddle-tank submarines have their main ballast tanks mounted externally as streamlined additions to the pressure hull (e.g. British Oberon-class SSK), with free-flooding holes at the bottom and vents at the top. A double-hull submarine has an outer hull surrounding the pressure hull over most of its length, the space between the two hulls being used for main ballast tanks and external fuel stowage.

Some submarines (like the Soviet Typhoon-class SSBN) have several pressure-hulls. These gigantic vessels have two complete, interconnected pressure hulls, each containing crew quarters and propulsion machinery, with a third, and smaller, pressurised section above and between them and directly under the sail for the command and control centre. Multiple-hull and saddle-tank arrangements have a valuable advantage in that weapon warheads exploding against the outer plates would have a certain amount of their explosive impact absorbed, thus reducing the effect on the pressure hull (this is similar to "spaced armour" on battle tanks).

Traditionally, high-yield steels have been used in submarine construction, but there is much research into stronger materials; titanium, aluminium and even glass have been considered. The US Navy currently uses HY-80 steel, while the Japanese use NS-90 in their Yuushio class; the French "Marel", a new high-tension steel, is claimed to give a 50 per cent increase in diving depth, and is being used in the latest French and Dutch submarines. The USSR has continued to use steel for the majority of its submarines, but at least two classes (Alfa and Mike) are known to be built of titanium. The Alfas are not only the world's fastest sub-

Above: The missile hatches on this American SSBN can be opened while submerged as an inner frangible seal prevents the missile tubes from flooding. During launch, a high-pressure air system shoots the missile through this seal to the surface, where the solid-fuel rocket takes over. The missile tube must withstand the pressure and stresses caused, both by this procedure, and the subsequent inrush of water. The first SSBNs presented unique challenges to submarine designers.

Above: A modern Swedish submarine under construction at the Kockums yard, with the stern section (foreground) ready to be mated with the main portion of the hull. Sweden is one of the relatively small number of nations which traditionally have designed and constructed submarines. However, there is a significant contemporary trend of more and more nations gaining the capability to construct their own conventional and nuclear-propelled submarines.

marines, but also the deepest diving, with estimates varying from 2,000ft (607m) to 3,000ft (914m). Titanium is a very difficult material to weld, although the Soviets — long acknowledged as world leaders in metallurgy — seem to have overcome this. Titanium has a further advantage in that it is non-magnetic and thus undetectable by devices such as airborne magnetic-anomaly detector (MAD) and bottom-laid coils. Titanium is, however, much ''stiffer'' than steel and if such a submarine is hit by a torpedo the force of the internal shock waves would cause severe damage.

Designers try to take all factors into account (e.g. variations in material characteristics, residual stresses, deviation in circularity, stress concentrations) in a ''Factor of Safety'', normally set between 1.5 and 2.0. This is used in the calculation: Collapse Depth (Design Depth) = Factor of Safety x Operational Depth. Thus, in a boat with a Factor of Safety of 1.74 (a typical figure) and an Operational Depth of 980ft (340m), Collapse Depth would be 1,705ft (520m).

Manoeuvrability

Manoeuvrability is important and modern control systems enable submarines to be "flown" three-dimensionally, like an aircraft. A turn within four times the submarine's length is possible and ascents/descents at rates of several hundreds of feet per minute are feasible, where water depth permits. Indeed, such aerodynamic problems as sideslip in turns have become important and the exact size, shape and position of the fin is also a critical factor.

Forward hydroplanes are used for diving and trimming, particularly at periscope depth. Most submarines are fitted with bow-mounted hydroplanes which either retract or fold and which pivot to achieve upward or downward motion. However, some navies (e.g. the American, Japanese and French) use sail-mounted planes, but these are unsuitable for use in the Arctic, which is a serious tactical limitation. Consequently, the US Navy recently announced that the planes will be moved to the bows on future Los Angeles and Seawolf-class SSNs. Submarines designed by the West German design bureau, Ingenieur Kontor Lloyd (IKL) (like the Type 209) have extendable, scythe-shaped bow hydroplanes, set at a fixed angle, with control being achieved by varying the total area exposed. The two planes are set at opposing angles — one is used when the vessel needs to descend, the other for ascent.

Most modern submarines have a cruciform (cross-shaped) stern empennage, with horizontal and vertical control surfaces and the propeller astern of them. In the American Los Angeles and Ohio classes the after horizontal hydroplanes are fitted with vertical endplates, both to improve control and also to serve as housings for hydrophones. The latest Swedish and Dutch classes, however, have an indexed, X-shaped empennage. First tested on USS *Albacore* (AGSS 569) this proved far superior, being more efficient in all major operating directions than a cruciform arrangement; it is also quieter and safer.

The submarine's greatest enemy is sonar and, apart from tactical methods of avoiding sonar detection, there are some passive measures which can be implemented at the design stage. One is to shape the contours of the hull in such a way that the sonar beams are diffused, a method which is analogous to the "stealth" technology now being applied to aircraft and to surface warships. Also, anechoic (sound absorbing) tiles can be used to coat the most critical parts of the submarine. These are already in use on Royal Navy and Soviet submarines and will be introduced by the US Navy on the next generation of attack submarines. The problems of tile adhesion remains to be solved, however.

Below: HMS Warspite, an SSN of the British Valiant class. Only the USA, USSR, UK, France and China currently have the technological capability to design and construct nuclear-powered submarines. However, India recently aquired a Soviet SSGN and has its own indigenous submarine construction capability, and Canada did seriously consider constructing SSNs. There are also persistent reports that other countries, in particular Argentina and Brazil, are seeking to construct their own SSNs. The current 'SSN club' may, therefore, expand in the forseeable future to include some new members.

Above: The helmsman's position on HMS Trafalgar, *one of the latest British SSNs. The spartan appearance of the interior of older submarines, with their myriad tubes and large wheels, is giving way to a more modern appearance as new* technology is brought to bear. The helmsman virtually 'flies' the submarine, controlling it 3-dimensionally, whereas in older submarines one man was responsible for depth control and another for direction.

Right: USS *Ohio (SSBN-726) lies at the Electric Boat Division Yard at Groton in Connecticut, USA. A second SSBN lies on the jetty to the left and clearly shows the vertical endplate on the after hydroplane. The Ohios are the first submarines to use such a device, which is used both to assist directional control and to house hydrophones. In front of* the construction hall is a circular hull section for an Ohio class submarine, which gives some indication of the huge internal volume of these boats. The Electric Boat Company, owned by General Dynamics, is the successor to the company founded by John Holland, builder of the first submarine, and builds most of America's submarines.

Propulsion

Of the many advances in submarine design, there can be no doubt that the greatest single post-war advance in submarine technology has been the advent of nuclear propulsion. This releases submarines from the vulnerable manoeuvre of coming near the surface to recharge batteries and replenish air supplies and gives almost limitless range.

Western nuclear-powered submarines use pressurised-water reactors (PWR). In the primary circuit, water under high pressure (to prevent it boiling and turning into steam) makes several passes through the nuclear reactor and thence to a steam generator. Here, heat energy is transferred to unpressurised water in the secondary circuit and the resulting steam then passes through the secondary circuit to the turbine. It is then turned into water again in a series of condensers and returns to the steam generator to recommence the cycle.

PWR condensers use seawater as a heat sink and require a constant throughput, either by the forward motion of the submarine or, at slow speeds, by the use of pumps. Pumping requires considerable electrical power, mainly to operate the circulation pumps in the primary circuit and the electric heater elements in the pressuriser. Free-circulation is used in USS *Narwhal* (SSN 671) with apparent success as it is now used in the S8G reactor in the Ohio-class SSBNs.

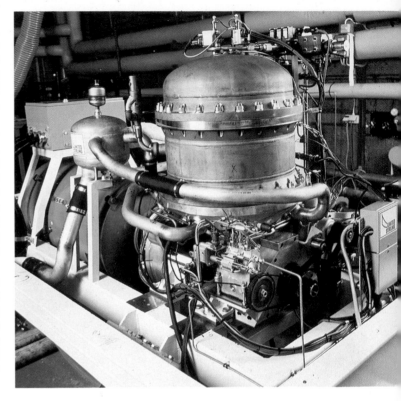

Pressurised-water nuclear propulsion system layout

Below: A pressurised-water nuclear propulsion system. Pressurised water in the primary circuit (red) heats cold water (blue) in the secondary circuit to steam (brown), which drives the turbines. Note the number of pumps in the various circuits; these are a source of noise which can be detected by sensitive listening devices.

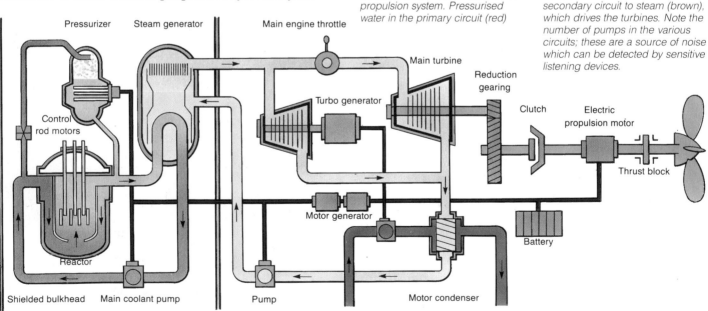

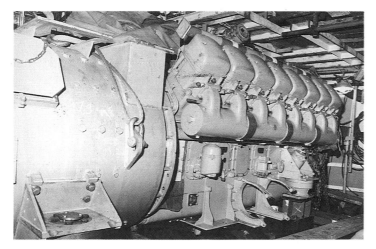

Left: The great weakness of the conventional diesel-electric submarine is that it must approach the surface regularly to 'snort'. A number of nations are now developing air-independent, non-nuclear propulsion systems. One such is the Stirling engine, seen here, now at sea in the Näcken, a converted Swedish submarine in a programme run by Kockums AB.

Above: A traditional diesel engine installation, in this case a SEMT-Pielstick A16 185 in an Agosta-class submarine built in France for the Pakistan Navy. Diesels do not transmit power direct to propellers, but power dynamos to charge the batteries, so that the same drive-system is always used. Note the very cramped space of this compact installation.

Other coolants have been tried. USS *Seawolf*, launched in 1955, used a liquid-sodium cooled reactor, giving much more efficient heat transfer, but it was troublesome in service and after two years was replaced by a PWR system. However, liquid-metal cooling seems to be the only way to obtain smaller, lighter plants and the Soviet Navy's high-speed Alfa class has such a reactor in a fully automatic, unmanned engine room.

A particular problem for nuclear-powered boats is that of machinery-generated noise, especially from gearing and rotating machinery such as pumps which, as described above, must be kept running. In most Western boats machinery is mounted on "rafts" in an effort to isolate the vibrations from the hull.

The final item in the drive-train is the propeller, a major cause of noise and one of the most readily identifiable features of individual submarines. Modern submarine propellers have up to seven blades, usually of a scythe shape and are designed to be run at very low revolutions. The latest British SSNs, however, are reported to use pump-jets, in which a ducted multi-bladed rotor turns against stator vanes, thus virtually eliminating cavitation noise, although much reduced rotating noises will probably still exist.

The Soviet Navy is reportedly examining a variety of other means of propulsion, including magnetohydrodynamic (MHD) generators and electrodynamic thrust (EMT). Both produce thrust without a propeller, thus avoiding cavitation and mechanical noise, and reducing wake turbulence.

In MHD an open, seawater-filled tube is surrounded by a ferro-liquid in a sealed sleeve. A pulsating magnetic field causes sympathetic vibrations in the ferro-liquid, setting up a travelling wave, which causes the water in the tube to be pumped out rearwards, imparting forward thrust to the submarine. This method of propulsion requires considerable electrical power and would only move the submarine slowly. Nevertheless, it would be valuable for moving the submarine in a virtually undetectable slow-speed cruise.

In EMT electro-magnets are mounted on the vessel's centre-line with banks of electrodes mounted down on either side of the ship. Electric current passing through the electrodes sets up a magnetic field and the action between the two magnetic fields results in forward motion. The USSR and Japan are both reported to be carrying out experiments with this type of system.

Diesel-electric submarines are far cheaper to build than nuclear submarines, are far less complicated to operate and avoid political problems associated with nuclear propulsion. However, they still must go to the surface to run their diesels and to recharge their batteries.

Closed-cycle systems are under constant consideration. The Brayton cycle uses inert gasses (argon, helium or xenon) as working fluids and was an unsuccessful competitor to power the US Navy's advanced lightweight torpedo (ALWT). Another device, the Stirling piston engine, is now under serious consideration by the Royal Swedish Navy and has been installed in a lengthened Näcken class submarine for operational tests.

Fuel cells also have potential for use in submarines. In such devices two chemicals combine in the presence of a catalyst, the reaction, which is usually fairly violent, being used for the direct production of electricity. Efficiency is high (up to 70 or 80 per cent in some cases), there are no severe heat dissipation problems, and, in many cases (e.g. a lithium/peroxide cell) the product is pure, potable water.

Batteries are heavy and space-consuming. Lead-acid batteries are cheap, simple to produce and relatively easy to maintain. Silver-zinc and silver-cadmium batteries are lighter, smaller and more efficient, but much more expensive and need more careful handling. Apart from constant research into new types of battery, much development effort is being put into improving the performance of lead-acid batteries, for example, by changing the electrolyte underwater to get rid of "poisoned" electrolyte.

Delta

The first really effective Soviet SSBN was the Yankee class, of which 34 were completed between 1967 and 1974. Carrying 16 SS-N-6 SLBMs these submarines have maintained patrols off the United States seaboard for many years, as witnessed only too dramatically in October 1986 when one surfaced east of Bermuda (and some 700nm (1,295km) from New York)

following an explosion. (It later sank in mid-Atlantic while being towed home.) Sixteen Yankee Is have had their missile tubes removed under the SALT-2 agreements and now serve as attack submarines (SSNs), except for one which has been rebuilt as a development boat for SS-NX-24 SLCMs. One other boat, the sole Yankee II, remains operational, carrying 12 SS-N-17 solid-fuelled SLBMs.

The Soviet SS-N-8 SLBM entered service in 1973, outranging Poseidon, at that time the latest United States

Below: The Delta-II entered service in 1972 and the basic design has been refined and lengthened through -II and -III to today's Delta-IV, shown here, which is still in production. Main weapons are 16 SS-N-23 ballistic missiles with a range of over 5,000nm.

Right: According to the USA the Delta-IV is designed to patrol under the Arctic ice, breaking through the ice in order to fire its missiles.

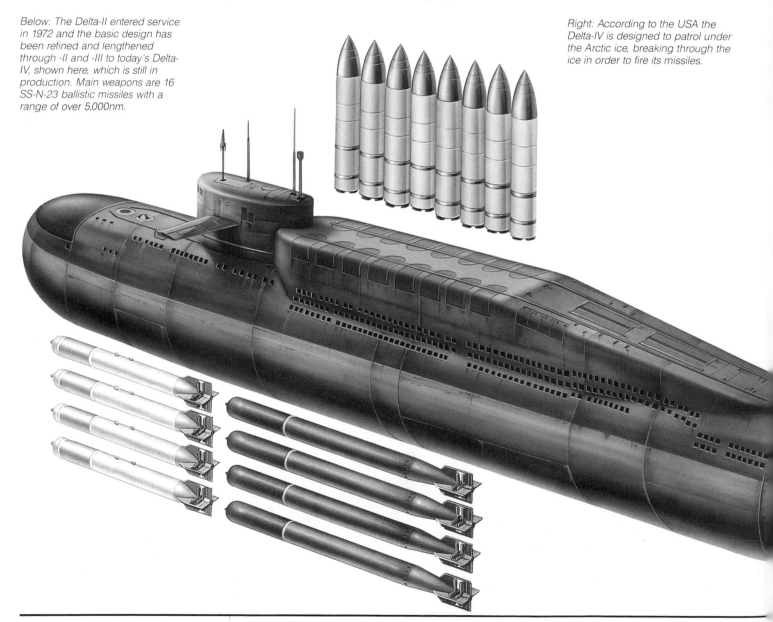

II. Sixteen two-stage SS-N-18 missiles are carried; these have a range of some 3,530nm (6,540km) and in the Mod. 3 version mount seven 200kT MIRVed warheads. Due to the greater length of the SS-N-18 missile the superstructure of the Delta III abaft the sail is even higher than that on Delta I and II and the hydrodynamic matching is very poor. This makes the Delta III very noisy, and it would be an easy target to detect and identify on passive sonar if it were to venture anywhere near a NATO ASW force.

Surprisingly, despite the commissioning of the first units of the Typhoon class in 1983, yet another new version of the Delta class — Delta IV — appeared in 1984. This carries 16 of another new Soviet Navy missile, SS-N-23, a replacement for SS-N-18, with a range of approximately 5,000nm (8,497km), armed with seven MIRVs. A fairing on the whaleback casing and a bracket further aft suggest that a towed array is used. The fin has also been modified and is now similar in height and outline to that fitted on the Oscar-class SSGN. Delta IV is designed for operations under the Arctic ice, breaking through the ice to launch its missiles.

It is clear from this progressive development that the Delta class has been successful. All these boats pose a significant threat to the United States, because they can hit North America from launching areas in the Sea of Okhotsk and the Barents Sea — the "SSBN sanctuaries" — where they are well out of range of any known countermeasures. Of the 38 Delta-class SSBNs in service, 23 are based with the Northern Fleet and 15 with the Pacific Fleet. However, as is normal Soviet Navy practice, only a small proportion of these submarines are on patrol at any one time.

It would seem that the Delta IV class is destined to remain in production for some time, although a replacement is almost certainly on the drawing board. The SS-N-23 SLBM may well be retrofitted to Delta III submarines, but it is too large for the Delta Is and IIs.

SLBM, although the Soviet missile, unlike its American counterpart, was not MIRVed (see later in text — SLBM) and used liquid fuel. Initial trials of the SS-N-8 were carried out in a converted Hotel III SSBN, but the missile first went to sea as an operational system in the new Delta I SSBN. This boat had been designed around the missile, although using the basic design of the earlier Yankee class as the starting point. Delta I is 459ft (140m) long and carries 12 missiles in two rows of six abaft the sail; it can be recognised by the step in the turtleback abaft the sail. Eighteen were built and all remain in front-line service.

Four Delta IIs, lengthened versions of the Delta I were then built, joining the fleet in 1975/76. The extra length, giving a total of 510ft (155m), enabled them to carry 16 SS-N-8 SLBMs, thus matching contemporary Western SSBNs.

Delta III, 498.7ft (150m) long, is slightly shorter than Delta

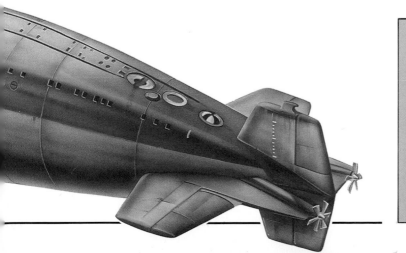

Origin: USSR.
Type: Ballistic-missile submarine, nuclear powered (SSBN).
Displacement: Surfaced 10,800 tons; submerged 13,500 tons.
Dimensions: 538 x 39.4 x 28.5ft (164 x 12 x 8.7m).
Performance: Maximum speed (submerged) 25 knots.
Maximum diving depth: Not known.
Machinery: Nuclear: Two pressurised water-cooled reactors driving steam turbines, 50,000shp. Propellers: Two seven-bladed.
Armament: Torpedo tubes: Six 21in (533mm) or 25.6in (650mm). Missiles: 16 SS-N-23 SLBM. Torpedoes: 18 conventional.
Complement: Not known.
Number in class: Delta I built, 18. Delta II built, 4. Delta III built, 14. Delta IV built, 4.
Constructed: 1970 onwards. If more being built is not known.
(Specifications apply to Delta IV.)

L'Inflexible

Origin: France.
Type: Ballistic-missile submarine, nuclear-powered (SSBN).
Displacement: Surfaced 8,080 tons; submerged 8,920 tons.
Dimensions: 422.5 x 34.9 x 32.9ft. (128.7 x 10.6 x 10m).
Performance: Maximum speed (submerged) 25 knots; (surfaced) 20 knots.
Maximum diving depth: Not known.
Machinery: Nuclear: One pressurised water-cooled reactor; geared steam turbines; 16,000hp. Electric: Emergency propulsion, range 5,000nm (9,350km). Propeller: One five-bladed.
Armament: Torpedo tubes: Four 21in (533mm). Missiles: 16 MSBS M-20 SLBM (first five boats). 16 M-4/TN-70 (*L'Inflexible* on building and all except *Le Foudroyant* during refit). Torpedoes: L-5 and L-7 torpedoes, and (in due course) SM39 missiles. Total 18.
Complement: 15 officers, 120 ratings.
Number in class: Built, 6.
Constructed: 1967 to 1985.

The French Navy currently possesses six SSBNs (French designation is SNLE). Five are of the Le Redoutable class constructed between 1964 and 1979, which are virtually identical with each other, while the latest, *L'Inflexible*, is of a modified design to incorporate the latest technological advances in propulsion, electronics and detection equipment. She can also dive 328ft (100m) deeper than the earlier boats and was built from the outset to take the new M-4 ballistic missiles.

As with the British, the French decided that it was necessary to build nuclear-powered ballistic missile submarines to ensure a viable national nuclear deterrent policy. Unlike the British, however, with their Polaris and Trident missile systems, the French "force d'dissuasion" has been developed virtually independently of the United States,

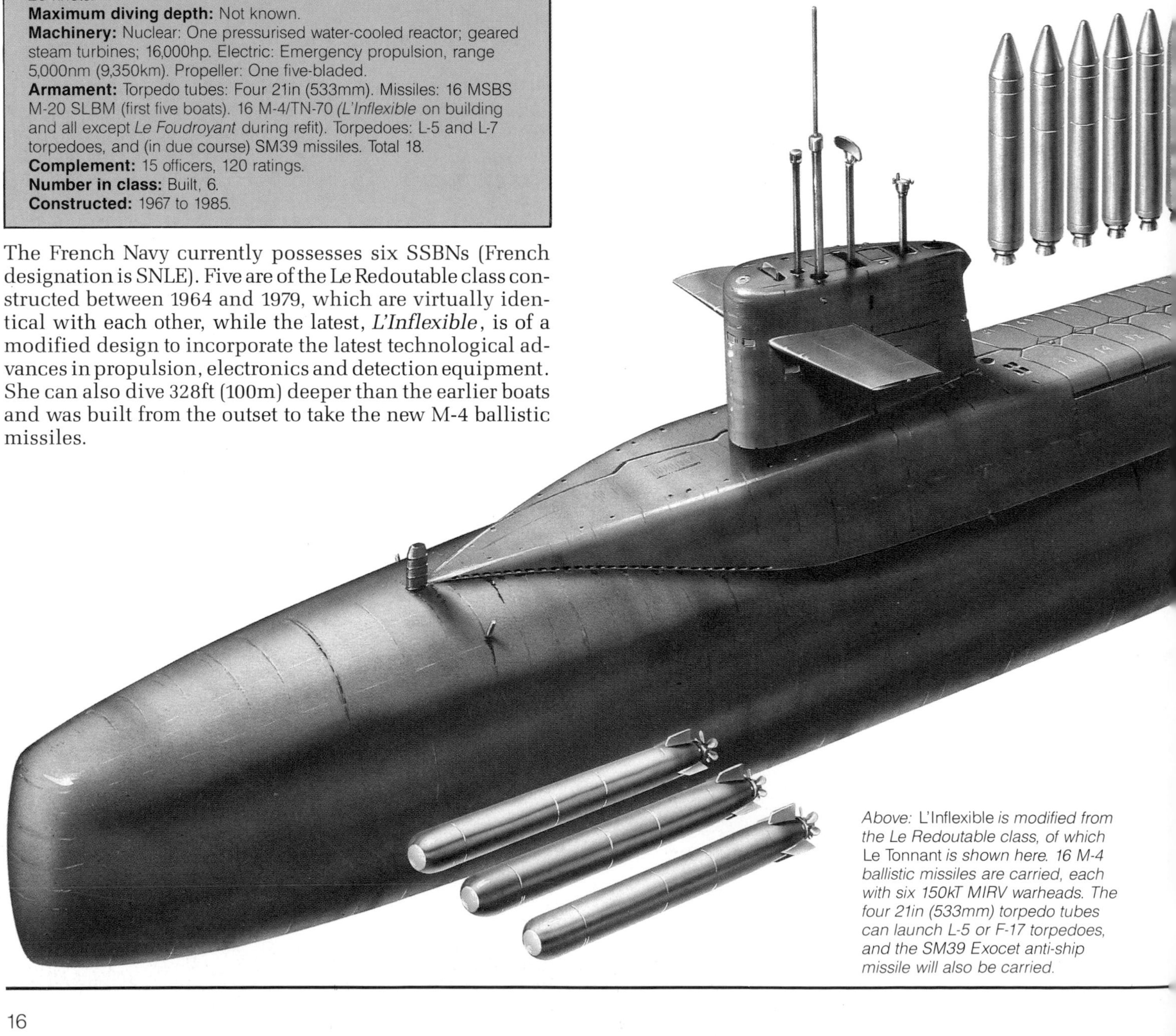

Above: L'Inflexible is modified from the Le Redoutable class, of which Le Tonnant is shown here. 16 M-4 ballistic missiles are carried, each with six 150kT MIRV warheads. The four 21in (533mm) torpedo tubes can launch L-5 or F-17 torpedoes, and the SM39 Exocet anti-ship missile will also be carried.

although some covert assistance may have been given. This has resulted in a much greater effort spread over a much longer timescale, and, at least in the earlier days, in heavier missiles carrying smaller warheads over shorter ranges.

The original Le Redoutable-class SSBNs were built to the same design philosophy as the American SSBNs in that they have two rows of eight missiles abaft the sail. However, unlike the Americans and the British, the French did not already have SSN designs which could be lengthened to accommodate the missile section. The French SSBNs have pressurised water-cooled nuclear reactors and turbo-electric

propulsion. They also have two auxiliary diesels that can be cut-in to provide power should the primary system fail; sufficient fuel is carried for 5,000 miles (8,046km). The forward hydroplanes are mounted on the fin, following the design of the US Navy SSBNs.

French policy is to have three SSBN hulls available at any one time, of which two must be on patrol. To achieve this the sixth boat, L'Inflexible, was ordered in 1979 and entered service in 1985. It is of an ''interim'' design, which is essentially an improved Le Redoutable, incorporating a number of modifications based on experience with the earlier boats and on recent technological developments.

The French Navy has had tactical problems as a result of the short range of the earlier types of missile. The Mer-Sol Ballistique Strategic (MSBS) M-1 SLBM, for example, which was fitted in the first two boats had a range of only 1,295nm (2,400km), but this has been progressively increased in successive missile systems. The first four boats were all modified to take the MSBS M-2 and have subsequently been modified again to take the M-20. The fifth boat was constructed from the outset to take the latter missile.

An even better missile — the M-4 — with a MIRVed warhead entered service in 1985 on L'Inflexible. This has a range in excess of 2,158nm (4,000km) and is armed with six of the new 150kT TN70 warheads. All boats have been altered to take this missile during long refits, except for the first, Le Redoutable, which is considered too old.

All boats are also armed with four 21in (533mm) bow-mounted torpedo tubes. The first five boats carry 18 torpedoes/SSMs, but L'Inflexible carries only 12.

Right: L'Inflexible *is seen during constructors trials, before being handed over to the French Navy. This boat is regarded as an intermediate stage between the original Le Redoutable boats and the next class of French SSBNs. The Le Triomphant class will enter service in the mid-1990s and will have a displacement of over 14,200 tons with a much greater diving capability than the current vessels. Continuing investment in SSBNs signifies French determination to maintain a completely independent nuclear deterrent.*

Ohio

Origin: United States.
Type: Ballistic-missile submarine, nuclear powered (SSBN).
Displacement: Surfaced 16,600 tons; submerged 18,700 tons.
Dimensions: 560 x 42 x 35.5ft (170.7 x 12.8 x 10.8m).
Performance: Maximum speed (submerged) 30+knots.
Maximum diving depth: 984ft (300m).
Machinery: Nuclear: One pressurised water-cooled S8G reactor; two geared turbines, 60,000shp. Propeller: One seven-bladed.
Armament: Torpedo tubes: Four 21in (533mm). Missiles: 24 tubes for Trident I (C-4) or Trident II (D-5) SLBM.
Complement: 15 officers, 142 ratings.
Number in class: Built, 10; building, 5; ordered, 5.
Constructed: 1976 and onwards to 1998.

Below: The scene at the Electric Boat Company yard, with Ohios in various stages of completion and a Los Angeles class SSN being launched.

While the US Navy programme of upgrading the later Polaris SLBM submarines to carry Poseidon was under way in the early — 1970s, development of an entirely new missile was started. This missile — Trident I C-4 — has a range of 3,830nm (7,100km), and is now in service aboard 12 converted Lafayette-class SSBNs, which were originally built to take the Poseidon C-3 SLBM (another 16 Lafayette-class boats remain in service with Poseidon missiles).

It was decided that in order to take full advantage of these

Left: The missile deck of an Ohio class SSBN with the missile hatches open. Each tube contains a Trident-I (C-4) missile weighing 31.65tons (32.26t) at launch, with a range of 4,350nm armed with eight 100KT MIRV warheads. The new Trident II (D-5) enters service in the 1990s.

missiles (and to accept the already-planned and slightly larger successor — Trident II D-5), a new class of larger SSBNs should be built. At first it was intended that these would be improved and enlarged Lafayettes, using the same Westinghouse SW5 pressurised-water reactor. There was, however, a pressing need to reduce noise levels as much as possible and it was decided to install an S8G natural-circulation reactor, based on the S5G which had been successfully tested in USS *Narwhal* (SSN 671). The S8G drives two sets of turbines — one for high-speed and the other for low-speed — and all machinery is mounted on noise-insulating rafts. It was also decided that it would be more cost-effective to design the new boats to take 24 missiles rather than 16, a payload increase of 50 per cent.

The US Congress baulked at the enormous cost of the new system, but when the Soviet Navy introduced its own long-range SLBM — the 3,650nm (6,760km) SS-N-8 in the Delta class — American reaction was to authorise and speed up the Trident programme, the first of the Ohio-class boats being laid down April 10, 1976. The first ten of these purpose-built Trident submarines have joined the fleet and ten more have been authorised.

The eventual number of Trident-carrying submarines depends upon two principal factors. The first is the outcome of the Strategic Arms Reduction Talks (START) between the United States and the USSR, and the other is expense. However, current US Navy plans are for a force of 20 Ohios, of which half would be allocated to the Pacific and Atlantic Fleets respectively. With an anticipated availability of 66 per cent, these boats will carry out 70-day patrols, followed by a 25-day short refit period. Each boat will have a full 12-month refit every nine years.

The first eight Ohio-class SSBNs (SSBN 726 to SSBN 733) are armed with 24 Trident I (C-4) missiles, mounted vertically abaft the sail. The Trident II (D-5) missile is being deployed on new Ohio-class SSBNs starting from the ninth (USS *Tennessee* (SSBN 734)) and will be retrofitted into the first eight. The D-5 cannot, however, be backfitted to the converted Lafayettes, now armed with Trident I (C-4). Trident II (D-5) carries larger payloads and is more accurate than Trident I, thus providing the SSBN force with the potential to put ''hard'' targets at risk, a significant expansion of the SSBN/SLBM role, which up to now has been as a survivable, second-strike, counter-value, deterrent system.

Ohio-class SSBNs also have four torpedo tubes firing conventional torpedoes and mounted below the sail. Extra tubes also fire ''countermeasure'' devices. Sensors include the BQQ-5 sonar system in the bows and a passive tactical-towed sonar array, for which the cable and winch are mounted in the ballast tanks. The array itself is housed in a prominent

Above: USS Georgia *(SSBN-729), the fourth of the class to be completed. SSBNs remain on the surface only to leave or enter port; their natural habitat is in the depths of the ocean.*

Right Top; First of class USS Ohio *(SSBN-726). The four circular ports in the hull below the sail are for ''countermeasures launchers'' (there are four more on the port side), devices to frustrate and confuse hostile ASW.*

Right: USS Ohio *(SSBN-726) running at very low speed on the surface. On a normal patrol she would cruise at a speed of some 3 knots at a depth selected by her captain to make best use of prevailing oceanic conditions.*

Left: The deterrence capability of an SSBN rests upon its ability to fire its missiles if necessary. This picture shows two fire controllers of the USN carrying out a simulated missile firing drill during an exercise on board USS Ohio *(SSBN-726).*

fairing which runs almost the entire length of the hull. There is current debate in the United States about the position from the late-1990s onwards when the last of the modified Lafayettes will be retired. As always there is pressure to find a less expensive alternative, which is not surprising in view of the cost of an Ohio-class SSBN — $1.8 billion per submarine in the 1985 budget. A further factor must be the possibility of a breakthrough in submarine detection (for example, from space-based sensors) which would deprive SSBNs of their current relative immunity.

The great advantage of the current generation of American and Soviet SLBMs is that they can be launched from their respective home waters. This makes detection of the launch platform and destruction of the submarine or the missiles very difficult, if not virtually impossible, which enhances their deterrent role. This great increase in missile range has also enabled the US Navy to operate the Ohio-class SSBNs from home ports in the contiguous United States. The first eight operate from Bangor in Washington State and the remainder out of King's Bay, Georgia.

Resolution

In 1962, President Kennedy agreed at the Nassau Conference to provide Polaris A-3 missiles for installation on British-built SSBNs. An important feature of this agreement was that the British would provide the nuclear warheads and re-entry vehicles, thus enabling them to retain national control over the use and targetting of the missiles.

Four submarines were built of an originally planned total of five, the last boat being cancelled in the Labour government's Defence Review in 1965. Much technical assistance was obtained from the United States although the actual design of *Resolution* was developed from that of the British Valiant-class SSNs, but with a missile compartment added between the control centre and the reactor room. The first boat was commissioned on October 2, 1967 and the fourth and last on December 4, 1969.

The Resolution-class SSBNs have 16 vertically-mounted missile launch tubes abaft the sail, containing Polaris missiles. The actual missiles are Polaris A-3s purchased from the United States, but, due to age-related deterioration, these have recently had to be fitted with new rocket motors, a very expensive undertaking, since the production lines had to be reopened and 1960s technology used.

The three re-entry vehicles (RVs) have also been totally replaced to overcome the effects of updated Soviet defences. Because of the national requirement for targetting autonomy the British undertook this as a national programme, codenamed *Chevaline*, at a cost of some £1,000 million. The total number of the new manouevrable re-entry vehicles (MRVs) is classified but can be assessed as six per missile; the yield of individual MRVs has also not been announced but is probably about 150kT. Chevaline may also include decoys to help penetrate Soviet defences.

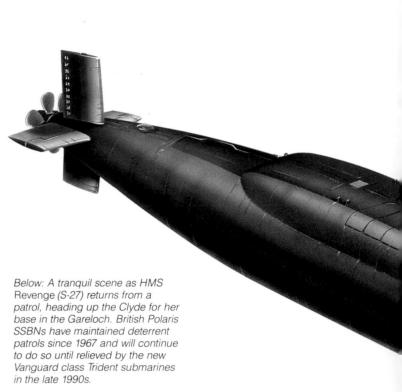

Below: A tranquil scene as HMS Revenge (S-27) returns from a patrol, heading up the Clyde for her base in the Gareloch. British Polaris SSBNs have maintained deterrent patrols since 1967 and will continue to do so until relieved by the new Vanguard class Trident submarines in the late 1990s.

Origin: United Kingdom.
Type: Ballistic-missile submarine, nuclear-powered (SSBN).
Displacement: Surfaced 7,600 tons; submerged 8,500 tons.
Dimensions: 425 x 33 x 30ft (129.5 x 10.1 x 9.1m).
Performance: Maximum speed (submerged) 25 knots; (surfaced) 20 knots.
Maximum diving depth: Not known.
Machinery: Nuclear: One Rolls-Royce PWR-1 pressurised water-cooled reactor; geared steam turbines; 15,000shp. Diesel: One generator for emergency power. Propeller: One.
Armament: Torpedo tubes: Six 21in (533mm). Missiles: 16 Polaris A-3TK SLBM.
Complement: 156 officers and ratings.
Number in class: Four in service.
Constructed: 1966 to 1969.

Right: HMS Resolution *(S-22) name ship of a class of four British SSBNs; a fifth boat was cancelled. They are armed with Polaris A-3TK SLBMs with British warheads, codenamed Chevaline.*

Following prolonged debate, which included detailed consideration of a variety of alternatives, the British government announced its intention to purchase Trident II (D-5) missiles from the United States. As with Polaris, an entirely British front-end is being fitted, thus ensuring national control of the system. The new missiles will be deployed in a new class of British-designed and built SSBN. Four of these Vanguard-class SSBNs are being built and, as far as is known, there are no plans to build a fifth.

Above: Resolution class SSBN of the Royal Navy. The Resolutions have 16 vertical launch tubes abaft the sail for their Polaris A-3TK missiles, each of which is armed with six 150kT warheads. Range is 2,500nm (4,600km). There are also six 21in (533mm) torpedo tubes in the bow, which are now equipped with Tigerfish wire-guided torpedoes, which have (at last) replaced the old Mark 8 torpedoes. Design of these RN SSBNs is similar to that of the US Navy's Lafayette class, except that bow planes are used.

Typhoon

Persistent rumours in Western naval circles about a new Soviet giant submarine were confirmed in November 1980. NATO announced that the USSR had launched the first of the Typhoon-class SSBNs. This event created great interest, not only because the Typhoon was the first totally new Soviet SSBN design for 20 years, but also because of the sheer size of this enormous craft. Its submerged displacement of 25,000 tons and overall length of 561ft (171m) made it by far the largest submarine ever built.

Among many unusual features of the Typhoon design is the 78.74ft (24m) beam; the normal length: beam ratio in SSBNs is in the region of 13:1, but the extraordinary girth of the Typhoon reduces this to 7:1. At first this was thought to indicate a considerable degree of separation between concentric outer and inner hulls, or simply a huge inner hull. It is now agreed, however, that the most probable explanation is that the single outer hull encloses two separate side-by-side pressure hulls, containing the propulsion and missile units, with a third pressure hull above them at the foot of the sail containing the control centre and a fourth pressure hull

Above: The mightiest of them all, the Typhoon class SSBN is, by a very considerable margin, the largest underwater vessel ever built. Armament is the SS-N-20 (Soviet designation RSM-52). Twenty of these are carried, the first solid-fuel SLBM to be produced in quantity for the Soviet Navy (the other solid fuel missile — SS-N-17 — is used only on the sole Yankee-II). SS-N-20 carries 6-9 MIRV warheads, with a maximum range of some 4,300nm.

Note that, unlike all other SSBNs, the Typhoon's missile launch tubes are located ahead of the sail, the reason for which is still not clear to Western experts. The precise number of torpedo tubes is also uncertain, but is thought to be six or eight, probably a mix of 21in (533mm) and 25.6in (650mm). Due to the vast size of the hull it is possible that as many as 40 torpedoes or other tube-launched missiles are carried as reloads.

Origin: USSR.
Type: Ballistic-missile submarine, nuclear powered.
Displacement: Surfaced 18,500 tons; submerged 25,000 tons.
Dimensions: 561 x 78.74 x 41ft (171 x 24 x 12.5m).
Performance: Maximum speed (submerged) 25 knots.
Maximum diving depth: Not known.
Machinery: Nuclear: Two 330-360MW pressurised water-cooled reactors. Propellers: Two seven-bladed.
Armament: Torpedo tubes: Six or eight 21in (533mm) or 25.6in (650mm). Missiles: 20 SS-N-20 SLBM. Torpedoes: 21in (533mm) or SS-N-15/16 ASW missiles.
Complement: 150 officers and ratings.
Number in class: Built, 5; building, 3.
Constructed: 1975 and onwards to 1995.

forward of these containing the torpedo tubes.

The principal armament of the Typhoon is its 20 SS-N-20 SLBMs located in launching canisters forward of the fin in two rows of ten; the SS-N-20 has six to nine MIRVed warheads and a range of 5,157 miles (8,300km). A battery of torpedo tubes is located forward of the missile compartment and, apart from conventional torpedoes, these may well be used for cruise missiles (e.g. SS-N-21) and minelaying; both weapons would be very useful if the Typhoon's role is in distant waters. One advantage of the Typhoon's unique layout is that all weapons are concentrated in one integrated area forward of the combat control centre.

If this submarine was to venture out into the open oceans it would seem to be relatively easy for opposing ASW forces to detect — its very size facilitates detection by many means. Conversely, the large volume of the hull makes quietening, a major problem in SSBN design, rather easier. One possibility would seem to be that the Typhoon is simply intended to be a relatively invulnerable missile-launching platform, re-

quired only to move out a short distance across the Barents Sea to the Arctic ice-cap and to loiter there, its time on station limited only by the endurance of the crew. For the latter role conditions can be assumed to be more spacious and comfortable than in any previous SSBN. There is, however, one other possibility: that the Typhoon is designed to operate for protracted periods a long way from its bases. The 4,500 mile (7,240km) range of its SS-N-20 SLBMs would certainly make it feasible for the Typhoon to operate in the southern oceans, thus posing a threat to the United States from completely new directions, and causing an expensive realignment of American warning and detection radar systems.

The sheer size of the Typhoon causes much comment in the West. However, it is worth noting that the Soviets have frequently exhibited a fascination with size and have built extremely large aircraft and ships for many years. For example, their latest ship classes of battlecruiser (Kirov), aircraft carrier (Kiev), SSGN (Oscar) and the Typhoon — all seem to fit in with this general pattern.

Left: Typhoon moves slowly and majestically on the surface, off the coast of the USSR. The cylinder at the base of the sail is thought to be a third, smaller pressure-hull housing the command centre. The coating of anechoic tiles, needed to prevent the transmission of sounds emanating from the interior (eg, circulation pumps), can be clearly seen, especially where there are some missing. The three raised triangular hatches are thought to cover housings for television cameras. This huge submarine is only marginally smaller than the battleships which fought at the Battle of Jutland in 1916, but the power of her nuclear weaponry is infinitely greater than all of those ships combined.

Xia

Origin: People's Republic of China (PRC).
Type: Ballistic-missile submarine, nuclear powered (SSBN).
Displacement: Submerged 7,000 tons.
Dimensions: 393 x 32.8 x ?ft (120 x 10 x ?m).
Performance: Maximum speed (submerged) 20 knots.
Maximum diving depth: Not known.
Machinery: Nuclear: One pressurised water-cooled reactor. Electric:
Turbo-electric drive. Propeller: One.
Armament: Torpedo tubes: Six or eight 21in (533mm) (estimate).
Missiles: 12 CSS-N-3 SLBM. Torpedoes: 12 21in (533mm) (estimate).
Complement: Not known.
Number in class: Built, 2; building, 2(+).
Constructed: 1982 onwards.

It has been known for some years in Western circles, that the People's Republic of China (PRC) had two parallel programmes in train to develop both a nuclear-power plant and a submarine-launched ballistic-missile (SLBM). The USSR gave the PRC the plans for a Golf class, diesel-electric powered, ballistic-missile submarine (SSB) in the 1950s, at a time when relations between the two countries were good. This led to the sole Chinese Golf-class submarine, which was built at the Huludao Yard and completed, after considerable delays, in the late-1970s. The Golf has three vertical missile tubes in the sail and was used for the PRC Navy's first successful submerged SLBM launch on October 12, 1982, when a CSS-NX-3 travelled a distance of 858nm (1,600km).

Subsequently, the existence of the SSBN necessary to make the system viable has been revealed. Nicknamed the "Xia" class by the West, this submarine has a displacement of 7,000 tons submerged and carries 12 CSS-N-3 SLBMs. Launched in April 1981 it is the product of a major national programme which seems to have been very successful. Rumours have circulated in the West of explosions of missiles and submarines, but these seem to have been products of wishful thinking, rather than based on fact. Constructed in the same yard as the Golf-class SSB and the Han-class SSNs at Huludao, some 125 miles (200km) north-east of Peking, two Xia-class boats are already at sea and a third and fourth will join them shortly.

The CSS-N-3 has a two-stage solid-fuel propulsion system and has a range of 1,500nm (2,795km). This certainly brings many targets in the Soviet Far East, such as ports, naval bases, airfields, C³ (command, control and communications) centres and strategic missile fields, within range, but it will not be until the next generation of SLBMs that the Chinese will be able to target the Soviet heartlands from submarines at sea. The Soviets know, however, that at the present rate of progress, that day is not far off.

Above: This picture is the only unclassified photograph so far released of the Xia class SSBN. It shows a configuration similar to the early American SSBNs, with two rows of six missiles under the raised decking behind the sail. Also following American practice, the Xia has the forward hydroplanes mounted on the sail. As it is unlikely that the Xia will operate under ice, this is no disadvantage. The Xia class should provide China with a secure maritime-based deterrence force, and it is assumed her SLBM deployment policy will be similar to that of the UK and France.

Charlie

The Soviet cruise-missile submarine programme started with some crude conversions of the diesel-electric Whiskey class (Whiskey Twin-Cylinder and Whiskey Long-Bin). The next generation appear to have been the result of a twin-track programme, with the nuclear-propelled Echo SSGNs and conventionally-powered Juliett-class SSGs. The SSGN progression then moved on to the Charlie class. Both the Echo and the contemporary November-class SSNs had hulls of the old, long, thin design, which made them slow, difficult to manoeuvre (especially at any speed), and cramped internally. As a result of considerable research (aided not a little by the fruits of espionage on United States and British naval establishments) the next generation of Soviet submarines was much "fatter" in relation to their length, and the Victor I SSN and Charlie I SSGN have remarkably similar dimensions.

The Echos and Julietts have their SS-N-3 cruise missiles installed in bins which must be raised to launch. There are also large wells to deflect the rocket efflux, which cause im-

Origin: USSR.
Type: Cruise-missile submarine, nuclear powered (SSGN).
Displacement: Surfaced 4,300 tons; submerged 5,500 tons.
Dimensions: 335 x 33 x 26ft (102 x 10 x 8m).
Performance: Maximum speed (submerged) 24 knots.
Maximum diving depth: 1,312ft (400m).
Machinery: Nuclear: One pressurised water-cooled reactor; steam turbines. Propeller: One seven-bladed.
Armament: Torpedo tubes: Six 21in (533mm). Missiles: 8 SS-N-9 or conventional torpedoes.
Complement: 90 officers and ratings.
Number in class: Charlie I built, 9. Charlie II built, 6.
Constructed: Not known.
(Specifications apply to Charlie II).

mense hydrodynamic drag as well as causing a considerable amount of noise. The installation in the Charlie class is much neater, with the missile launch tubes being located in the bow between the inner and outer hulls, and covered by large square hatches, which are fully smoothed into the streamlined outer casing to reduce drag and noise.

Charlie Is were built at a rate of about two per year from

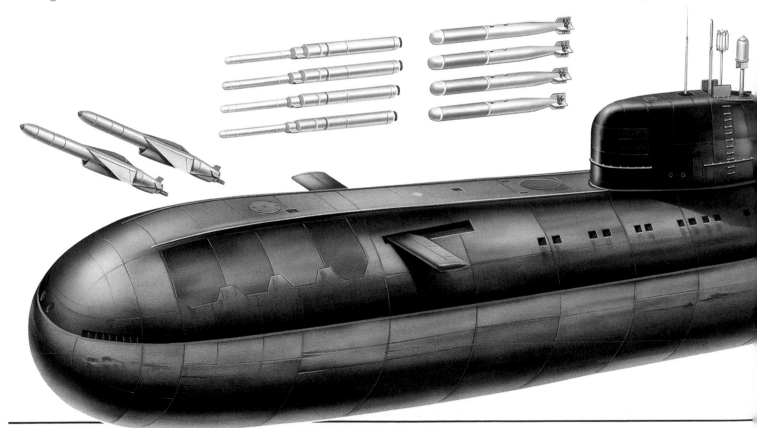

Above: Charlie-I class SSGN are armed with eight SS-N-7 submarine-launched cruise missiles and their mission in war would be to attack

NATO task groups in the North Atlantic. The threat that these SSGNs pose is taken very seriously by NATO fleet commanders.

1968 to 1973. They are 308.4ft (94m) long, with a submerged displacement of 5,000 tons. Charlie I is armed with eight SS-N-7 cruise missiles which are launched from underwater and have a range of 35nm (49km). They carry either conventional or nuclear warheads. They seem to have been fairly reliable in service, although one sank in June 1983 in the Pacific. It was subsequently raised by the Soviet Navy and returned to the USSR, but it does not appear to have been returned to service.

The Charlie II appeared in 1973 and is 23ft (7m) longer, an additional hull section having been added between the sail and the missile tubes. Charlie II is armed with eight of the more advanced SS-N-9 missiles, which have inertial guidance and active radar homing; they are also launched from underwater.

The principal role of the Charlie-class SSGNs is to attack NATO battle groups, particularly those centred on strike carriers. Most of the Charlie Is and all the Charlie IIs serve with the Northern Fleet and would operate in the North Atlantic in a general war.

In a unique move, one Charlie I has been lent to the Indian Navy, arriving there on January 5, 1988, the first ever occasion in which one nation has lent a nuclear-powered submarine to another. It is believed that this loan is to enable the Indian Navy to gain expertise in operating nuclear submarines prior to the delivery of more up-to-date boats, possibly Victor III SSNs.

Below: The Soviet Navy's Charlie-I class SSGN entered service between 1968 and 1971. Ten were built, of which one sank in the Pacific in 1983. One was lent to the

Indian Navy on 5 January 1988, the first time a nuclear-propelled submarine of any kind has been lent to a Third World navy by a nuclear-equipped superpower.

Above: Charlie II class SSGN, armed with eight SS-N-9 SLCM. This missile is fitted with inertial guidance with active radar homing onto the target, and carries either a conventional or a nuclear warhead. Charlie II also carries twelve tube-launched SS-N-15 missiles as well as conventional torpedoes.

Oscar

The year 1980 saw the launching of two Soviet navy giants: the Typhoon-class SSBN and the Oscar-class SSGN. The first two of the Oscar class (Oscar I) have a surfaced displacement of 11,500 tons and submerged of 14,500 tons, and a length of 479ft (146m). The third and subsequent Oscars (Oscar II) are 32.8ft (10m) longer; this does not appear to result in a greater weapon load, but must give increased interior volume for C^3 facilities or living-space. The exceptionally broad-beamed hull is covered with anechoic tiles, although these seem to be inadequately secured, as most photographs show a number missing.

All Oscars are armed with 24 SS-N-19, an anti-ship cruise missile (ASCM) capable of being fired from underwater, and at least six torpedo tubes — although there appears to be room in the massive hull for plenty more. With a submerged speed well in excess of 30 knots an Oscar-class SSGN could operate as the advance guard of a Soviet task group, capable of attacking major surface combatants out to a range of 170 to 215nm (322 to 402km).

The Oscar-class boats have an excellent combination of sensors and missile systems, coupled with high speed and good survivability. Thus, one of the roles they may be able to undertake is that of distant-water, independent operations, possibly as a modern, underwater, equivalent of the German "commerce raider" pocket battleships of World War II.

However, it must be assumed that the primary role of the SSGN in the Soviet Navy is that of attacking NATO carrier task groups. In this case, the Oscar class is most probably a Soviet counter to the increased protection afforded to US Navy carrier groups by Los Angeles-class SSNs and carrier-borne Lockheed S-3 Viking ASW aircraft.

Above: This excellent overhead shot shows the virtually hemispherical shape of the Oscar's bow, a design adopted after extensive research into the hydrodynamics of large marine creatures, such as whales. Clever shaping ensures high speed with low noise generation.

The increased firepower required to overcome the carrier group's defences is provided by the SS-N-19, which has an estimated range of 200 to 250nm (375 to 465km). The missile itself is estimated to be some 32ft (10m) long and is launched from a tube angled at 45°. The large quantity of missiles fitted to the Oscar-class SSGNs suggests that such an attack might be launched with several missiles, with the intention of overwhelming the task group defences by sheer weight of numbers.

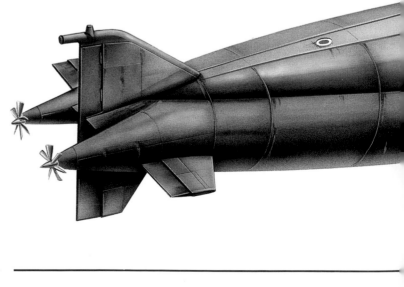

Origin: USSR.
Type: Cruise-missile submarine, nuclear powered (SSGN).
Displacement: Surfaced 13,000 tons; submerged 16,000 tons.
Dimensions: 512 x 59 x 32.8ft (156 x 18 x 10m).
Performance: Maximum speed (submerged) 33 knots.
Maximum diving depth: Not known.
Machinery: Nuclear: Two pressurised water-cooled reactors. Propellers: Two seven-bladed.
Armament: Torpedo tubes: Six 21in (533mm) or 25.6in (650mm). Missiles: 24 SS-N-19 ASCM. Torpedoes: 24 SS-N-15/16 ASW missiles or torpedoes.
Complement: 130 officers and ratings.
Number in class: Oscar I built, 2. Oscar II built, 2.
Constructed: 1982 onwards and possible six under construction up to 1990.
(Specification applies to Oscar II; Oscar I is slightly different.)

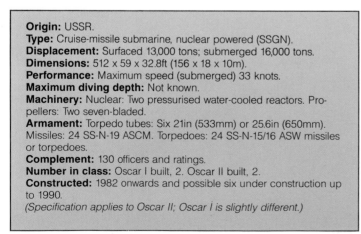

The Oscar-class submarines are double-hulled, with the missile launch tubes mounted between the inner and outer hulls, 12 on each side. The hull is of the usual Soviet shape but much broader in profile, due to the location of the missile tubes. A prominent tube-shaped device on the tip of the vertical rudder is probably designed to be the mooring for a towed sonar array. Unusually among modern submarines, but like the Typhoons, the Oscar class are equipped with twin shafts and propellers.

Two Oscar Is and at least two Oscars IIs are known to have been completed. Although the development of long-range cruise missiles which can be launched from torpedo tubes, such as SS-NX- 21, enable almost any SSN to be employed as a cruise-missile launcher, it seems that the Soviet Navy is not yet ready to discontinue the production of specialised SSGNs such as the Oscar. The large salvo capability could pose severe problems to NATO.

Above: This Oscar SSGN has large numbers of anechoic tiles missing from the hull.

Below: The main armament of the Oscar is 24 SS-N-19 anti-ship cruise missiles, which are fired from angled launch tubes abeam the sail. Unlike other modern submarines (with the sole exception of the Typhoon class SSBN) the Oscar has twin propellers, a feature avoided in the West due to the inherent noise created by such a propulsion configuration.

Akula

Origin: USSR.
Type: Attack submarine, nuclear powered (SSN).
Displacement: Surfaced 7,500 tons; submerged 10,000 tons.
Dimensions: 370 x 42.65 x 32.8ft (113 x 13 x 10m).
Performance: Maximum speed (submerged) 35 knots.
Maximum diving depth: Approximately 1,312ft (400m).
Machinery: Nuclear: Two pressurised water-cooled reactors; steam turbines. Shafts: One. Propeller: One seven-bladed.
Armament: Torpedo tubes: Six 25.6in (650mm) or 21in (533mm). Missiles: SS-N-15, SS-N-16, SS-N-21 SSMs or torpedoes.
Complement: Not known.
Number in class: Built, 3.
Constructed: 1981 onwards. Several are building presently.

Below: The Akula is significantly quieter than earlier Soviet SSNs, and gives a new attack capability to the Soviet Navy. Six 25.6in (650mm) or 21in (533mm) torpedo tubes can launch a wide range of ASW and anti-ship weapons. The SS-N-16 nuclear missile gives a powerful anti-submarine capability, backed up by homing torpedoes and the SS-N-16 torpedo carrying missile. Mines and anti-ship torpedoes can also be launched, and perhaps the SS-N-21 cruise missile.

Having used all the letters in its phonetic alphabet system for Soviet submarines (Alfa through Zulu), NATO has designated this latest SSN type "Akula", the Russian word for "shark". (The actual Soviet designation is, of course, not known.)

Soviet SSN design appears to be following two main strands: one is the Alfa-Mike-Sierra series and the other is the Victor-Akula series. The Victor I class first appeared in 1968 and a total of 16 boats were completed. Of 5,100 tons submerged displacement, they had an underwater speed of 30 knots and were armed with six 21in (533mm) torpedo tubes. They had one five-bladed main propeller and two (separate) small, two-bladed propellers for use during slow speed "creep" operations.

Next came seven Victor IIs, built between 1972 and 1978. Longer than the Victor I, they introduced the new Soviet 25.6in (650mm) torpedo tubes, with four such tubes in addition to two 21in (533mm) tubes.

The Victor III was longer still — 348ft (106m) compared to 312ft (95m) for the Victor I — and introduced the large teardrop-shaped pod atop the vertical rudder now seen on the Sierra and Akula classes, as well. Some Victor IIIs have a conventional seven-bladed propeller, but others have a unique eight-bladed device, consisting of two co-rotating, tandem, four-bladed propellers oriented at 22.5° to each other. Western experts had thought that the Victor III had been phased out of production in 1983 after 20 units had been completed, but two further boats were completed in 1985 and 1987. These may be intended for export, possibly to India who received a nuclear-powered Charlie I SSGN on loan in 1988.

The first Akula-class SSN was launched in 1984, the second in 1986 and the third in 1987. They are longer and broader than the Victor III class and, according to the US Department of Defense, they "demonstrate a level of quieting that is greater than previously anticipated" and are "the most capable attack submarines yet developed for the Soviet Navy". The quieting measures include the use of sound-insulation mountings (rafting) for the propulsion plant and anechoic coating of the steel hull.

There is considerable speculation in the West as to the purpose of the teardrop device atop the vertical rudder. One suggestion is that it is associated with a towed-array sonar, although this seems a complicated way of dealing with a requirement solved much more simply in other submarines. An alternative suggestion is that this fairing houses a MHD (see page 13) device for very quiet, slow-speed propulsion during silent "creep" operations.

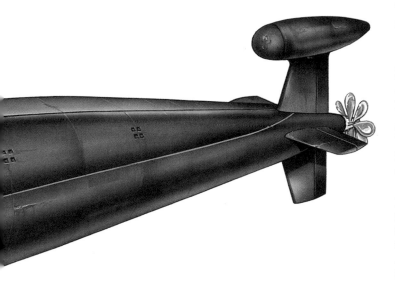

Right: Longer and wider than the Victor III boats, the Akulas have a similar configuration. Measures taken to reduce noise include anechoic tiles on the outside of the hull, and this picture shows that the problems of tile loss at sea have not yet been completely solved. It is not clear why the Soviet Union is bearing the enormous cost of simultaneous development of both the Sierra and Akula SSNs, but in the Akula the Soviet Navy has created an extremely effective attack submarine.

Los Angeles

The Los Angeles class is 45-strong today, building up to an eventual class total of 66, and is one of the most sophisticated, expensive, effective and important weapons systems in service today. Its origins go back to the late-1960s when the US Navy considered two classes of future SSNs: one was to be a high-speed attack and ASW submarine, and the second a very quiet type intended for "barrier" operations.

The latter requirement led to the USS *Glenard P. Lipscomb* (SSN 685), the outcome of a development programme for a "quiet" submarine which stretched back to USS *Tullibee* (SSN 597) of the early-1960s. *Lipscomb*, launched in 1973, has many interesting features aimed at achieving silent running, a number of which were subsequently incorporated into the Los Angeles class. *Lipscomb* is powered by a Westinghouse S5WA natural-circulation reactor driving a turbo-electric plant, a system which removes the requirement for extensive gearing, one of the prime sources of noise in nuclear submarine propulsion systems.

The first element of this programme, the high-speed ASW type, became the Los Angeles class and it was decided that, rather than go in for the considerable extra expense of two separate classes, the USS *Los Angeles* (SSN 688) could perform both roles. Although *Lipscomb* remains in front-line service, the turbo-electric drive system was not repeated in the Los Angeles class.

The Los Angeles boats are much larger than any previous United States SSN, being 57.8ft (17.63m) longer than the Sturgeon class, and the hull is optimised for high submerged speed and has a very small sail. One unfortunate outcome is that, because the sail-mounted planes cannot be rotated to the vertical, the *Los Angeles* cannot break through ice. This problem will be overcome from the USS *San Juan* (SSN 751)

Above: This unusual shot of a Los Angeles class SSN running on the surface shows the hull fairing which houses the towed sonar array.

Origin: United States.
Type: Attack submarine, nuclear powered (SSN).
Displacement: Surfaced 6,080 tons; submerged 6,900 tons.
Dimensions: 360 x 33 x 32.3ft (109.7 x 10.1 x 9.9m).
Performance: Maximum speed (submerged) 30 knots.
Maximum diving depth: 1,476ft (450m).
Machinery: Nuclear: One pressurised water-cooled S6G reactor; two geared turbines; 35,000shp. Propeller: One seven-bladed.
Armament: Torpedo tubes: Four 21in (533mm). Missile tubes: 16. Missiles: Conventional torpedoes, Subroc and Mark 48 A/S torpedoes. SSN 688 to SSN 720 also have tube-launched Tomahawk SLCM (22 reloads). Vertical Launch Tubes: 15 for Tomahawk SLCM from SSN 721 onwards.
Complement: 12 officers, 115 to 127 ratings.
Number in class: Built, 45; building, 14; ordered, 7.
Constructed: 1972 onwards and into the mid-1990s.

Left: Conditions in the operations room of Los Angeles class SSN, La Jolla (SSN-701), are comfortable and relaxed, in marked contrast to those in earlier vessels.

Left: The four midships 21in (533mm) torpedo tubes can fire the complete range of tube-launched weapons currently in US service: SUBROC, Sub-Harpoon, the dual-purpose Mk 48 torpedo, and the T-LAM and T-ASM versions of Tomahawk. However, submarines from SSN-719 onwards have twelve separate vertical launch tubes for Tomahawk mounted between the forward end of the pressure-hull and the spherical BQQ-5 sonar array in the bow. The first Los Angeles class boat was laid down in 1972 and the 66th and last will not be laid down until well into the 1990s, a record production run for any type of submarine. There have, of course, been many improvements during that period, but the basic, thoroughly sound design has remained constant throughout.

onwards, these boats having their diving-planes moved forward to the more traditional bow position. Together with some new electronic equipment this enables them to be declared "Arctic-capable".

The sensor fit is comprehensive and includes the BQQ-5 sonar system in the bow and a passive tactical towed sonar array. The cable and winch are mounted in the ballast tanks, but there is no room for the array itself, which is, therefore, housed in a prominent fairing which runs along almost the entire length of the hull.

The most remarkable feature of the Los Angeles class, however, is its armament. These powerful submarines are armed with Subroc and Sub-Harpoon, as well as conventional and wire-guided torpedoes. All boats from SSN 688 to SSN 718 carry up to eight Tomahawk missiles as part of their torpedo loads. All these are fired from the four 21in (533mm) torpedo tubes located amidships and angled outwards. From SSN 721 onwards, however, 15 vertical launch tubes for Tomahawk are being fitted in the space in the bow between the inner and outer hulls, thus restoring the torpedo capacity. So, although their primary mission is still to hunt other submarines and to protect SSBNs, the Los Angeles class can also be used without modification to sink surface ships at long-range with Sub-Harpoon, while Tomahawk enables them to operate against strategic targets well inland, as well. It has also been announced that from Fiscal Year 1985 the Los Angeles class will be given a mine-laying capability, increasing the flexibility of this weapons system.

The Reagan Administration ordered a speeding-up of the Los Angeles building programme; three boats were completed in 1986, two in 1987 and three in 1988 and the rate is now stabilising at three per year. The Tomahawk missile programme was also accelerated, with these missiles being fitted in USS *Providence* (SSN 719) onwards.

Left: USS Dallas *(SSN-700) launched at the GD, Electric Boat Division yard at Groton, Connecticut on 28 April 1979. The large star-spangled sheet covers the fibreglass bow, beneath which is the BQQ-5 sonar array.*

Below: USS Los Angeles *(SSN-688), name-ship of the class. Note how the wake characteristics are different to those of Soviet submarines, such as the Charlie class shown earlier.*

There has been much criticism of the complexity and cost of the Los Angeles class, and it is alleged that too many sacrifices were made to achieve the very high speed. A design for a cheaper and smaller SSN, under construction in 1980 as a result of Congressional pressure, was later shelved, but may well reappear, especially if the proposed new class should turn out to be even more expensive than the Los Angeles, which is highly possible. Meanwhile there are plans to improve the Los Angeles boats, especially their sensors, weapons systems and control equipment. Such improvements will include moving the torpedo tubes back to the bow, and increasing their number to eight. Further, at least some of the Los Angeles boats will also probably get anechoic coatings, the first to be given to a United States submarine.

The Los Angeles class is very sophisticated and each boat is an extremely potent fighting machine. With a production run of at least 66 it must be considered an outstandingly suc-cessful design. These boats are, however, becoming very expensive: the first cost $221.25 million, while the boat bought in 1979 cost $325.6 million, and the two in 1981 a massive $495.8 million for each vessel.

Design work has already started on the USS *Seawolf* (SSN 21) the name boat of the next major class of SSNs for the US Navy. Among the major objectives in this very important programme are even better sound quieting and a greater under-ice capability than the Los Angeles class, both being intended to challenge the Soviet SSBNs and SSNs operating under the Arctic ice-cap. A noteworthy development is that the forward hydroplanes will be mounted on the bow rather than on the sail. It is also planned that the Seawolf class will carry many more weapons than today's SSNs. Under present plans *Seawolf* will have eight torpedo tubes, with no less than 50 missiles, a mix of Sea Lance, Tomahawk, Sub-Harpoon, Mark 48 ADCAP torpedoes and mines.

Right: USS Honolulu *(SSN-718). These submarines are hunter-killers, intended to detect, track and then kill hostile SSBNs and SSNs. They have extremely high-grade sonar systems, although these cannot operate with maximum effectiveness when the submarine is travelling at over about 10 knots, due to the 'self-noise' created by the rush of water flowing over the hull. They tend to hunt enemy vessels therefore, using 'sprint-and-drift' tactics.*

Rubis

Origin: France.
Type: Attack submarine, nuclear powered (SSN).
Displacement: Surfaced 2,385 tons; submerged 2,670 tons.
Dimensions: 236.5 x 24.9 x 21ft (72.1 x 7.6 x 6.4m).
Performance: Maximum speed (submerged) 25 knots.
Maximum diving depth: 980ft (300m).
Machinery: Nuclear: One pressurised water-cooled reactor, 48MW two turbo-alternator sets. Electric: One main motor. Propeller: One seven-bladed.
Armament: Torpedo tubes: Four 21in (533mm). Missiles: L-17, L-5 Mod. 4 torpedoes or SM-39 Exocet missiles (total 14).
Complement: 9 officers, 57 ratings.
Number in class: Four in service.
Constructed: 1982 to 1987.

Below: The Rubis has four 21in (533mm) torpedo tubes with room to store 14 reloads. The wire-guided F-17 torpedo can be carried, as can the earlier acoustic homing L-5. The torpedo tubes can also launch TSM 3510 mines and a long range anti-ship capability is given by SM 39 Exocet anti-ship missiles.

France came late onto the SSN scene. Other nations developed their nuclear submarine fleets by first producing SSNs and then graduating, to SSBNs, since, in general terms, missile technology lagged behind that for nuclear-propulsion systems. France, under strong pressure from President de Gaulle, proceeded straight to SSBNs. Not surprisingly, such a massive programme, which, for political reasons, had to be entirely French in character, took up all the available resources for many years. It was not until the 1974 programme, therefore, that the French Navy was able to turn its attention to SSNs. The first of the class, *Rubis* (S 601) (originally named *Provence*), was laid down in December 1976 and launched July 7, 1979. She joined the fleet February 28, 1983 after extensive trials and has since been joined by the three remaining members of the class in 1984, 1987 and 1988.

The Rubis class are the smallest operational SSNs in any navy. The hull design is based fairly closely on the Agosta class of conventional submarines, but the Rubis is externally distinguishable on the surface by the larger sail and the horizontal diving planes set about two-thirds of the way up it. To be able to construct such a small nuclear-powered submarine suggests that the French Navy has achieved a significant development in nuclear reactor design, compared with

the rather large devices in the Le Redoutable-class SSBNs, and, indeed, with those in the SSNs of other nations. It was thought for some years that this had been achieved by the use of liquid metal cooling in the reactor, but it is, in fact, now confirmed that this reactor system is a conventional pressurised-water design.

Armament, sonar and fire-control systems were based on those in service in the Agosta class and, as with those boats, the torpedo tubes are the internationally standardised 21in (533mm), indicating a final abandonment of the French 21.7in (550mm) torpedo. *Saphir* (S 602), second in the class was the first to be fitted for SM-39 Exocet, an adaptation of the very successful MM-38 Exocet surface-launched anti-ship missile. Like the US Navy's Sub-Harpoon, SM-39 is tube-launched from a submerged submarine. *Rubis* (S 601) has since been modified to take SM-39.

Unlike other navies, the French Navy has two crews for each of these SSNs, each of 9 officers and 57 ratings; this ensures maximum utilisation of the hull. The average patrol is estimated to last 45 days.

The first of the next class of four boats was laid down in 1988 and will be commissioned in 1991. They are designated the Amethyst class, which is both the name of the first of the class and also the French acronym for *Amelioration Tactique Transmission Ecoute* (i.e. reduced radiation emission). These boats have been designed to be marginally larger than the Rubis class with a submerged displacement of 2,600 tons and a length of 241.5ft (73.6m).

Right: Experience gained during the SSBN programme enabled the French to design an extremely compact and effective SSN class. An integrated reactor-exchanger reduces the size and weight of the propulsion machinery, and allows a nuclear submarine to be built which is not much bigger than the Agosta SSK class. The French have also followed American practice in mounting the forward hydroplanes high on the sail, which protects them when docking.

Sierra

The first Soviet SSNs were the November class, which entered service between 1958 and 1963 and which had a long, inefficient hull with a multiplicity of free-flood holes, making them very noisy boats and thus relatively easy to detect. Several had accidents, including one which sank in the Western Approaches to the English Channel in April 1970. Next in production was the Victor class, which was a substantial step forward, with a "teardrop" hull and a new nuclear reactor system.

The spectacular Alfa class was next to appear. Constructed of titanium, these boats have a diving depth of 2,500ft (700m) and a submerged speed in excess of 42 knots, which they have demonstrated to spectacular effect whilst observing numerous NATO exercises. The first boat was completed in 1972 but was scrapped only two years later. Since then production has been slow but steady, suggesting that fabrication was difficult even for a country so advanced in the metallurgical field as the USSR.

The first boat of the Sierra class was launched in July 1983 and went to sea in 1984. It appears to be a successor to the Victor III class and may have a titanium hull. It has a similar "bullet" atop the vertical rudder to that on the Akula class; at first thought to be for a towed sonar array, it is now suggested that this may be for some form of propulsion, possibly

Above: Sierra class SSN. The cone-shaped device on the left-hand mast is a Pert Spring SATCOMM system antenna.

Left: Sierra-class SSN. The large mast with a bulky antenna is the Snoop Pair/Rim Hat radar, with EW antennas at its base. The large teardrop-shaped pod atop the vertical rudder also appears on Victor-III and Akula class SSNs, but its precise purpose has not yet been revealed. It may house the winch and reel for a towed array sonar system.

Origin: USSR.
Type: Attack submarine, nuclear powered (SSN).
Displacement: Surfaced 6,000 tons; submerged 7,550 tons.
Dimensions: 351 x 39.4 x 24ft (107 x 12 x 7.4m).
Performance: Maximum speed (submerged) 36 knots.
Maximum diving depth: Not known.
Machinery: Nuclear: Two pressurised water-cooled reactors, one steam turbine; approximately 40,000 shp. Propeller: One seven-bladed.
Armament: Not known.
Complement: Approximately 85 officers and ratings.
Number in class: Two in service; more building.
Constructed: 1981 onwards.

Below: The Sierra class SSN has six bow tubes, with a mix of 21in (533mm) and 26in (650mm) diameters. All weapons in the current inventory can be handled, including SS-N-15, -16, -21 and torpedoes. Building rate of the Sierra class is very slow; the first was launched in August 1983 and *the second some three years later; the third has yet to be reported. It is possible that this is a titanium-hulled successor to the Alfa-class, with the lengthy construction time indicating the difficulty of working this unusual metal. Maximum submerged speed is reported to be 36 knots, but could be much higher.*

associated with a MHD generator (see page 13). The forward hydroplanes have been moved further down on the bow and the fin is somewhat more angular, although markedly lower than in Western SSNs.

These are clearly very capable boats, being purpose-built for the ASW attack role. No Western expert is certain (at least in public) why the Soviet Navy is producing two types of nuclear-powered attack submarine (Akula and Sierra) simultaneously, with the (apparently) "one-off" Mike as a third path of development. One possible explanation is that the Mike class represents the "high technology" end of the spectrum, while the Sierra class is the "low technology" end, using tried and trusted techniques in a not very ambitious advance on the Victor III class. This would be similar to the approach used with the Kirov, the advanced battlecruiser design, and the much less revolutionary Slava class produced concurrently as a safeguard against failure. This insurance seems to have paid off, as no further Mikes have been built, and the sole example was sunk with heavy loss of life in April 1989, after an on-board fire.

Sturgeon

The US Navy's Sturgeon-class SSNs were slightly enlarged and much improved versions of the Permit (Thresher) design. Several interesting problems arose during the building of this class: USS *Pogy* (SSN 647) had to be allocated to another yard for completion, while USS *Guitarro* (SSN 665) was delayed for more than two years after sinking in 35ft (10.7m) of water during fitting-out. A Congressional committee later described this incident as "wholly avoidable".

Like the Permit class, the Sturgeons have an elongated teardrop hull with a large sonar in the bow. This is the BQQ-2 in the first 28 boats (SSN 637 to SSN 677), but the last nine boats to be built (SSN 678 to SSN 687) have the larger BQQ-5 sonar (as fitted in the Los Angeles class). They are, therefore, longer being 302.2ft (92.1m) compared to 292ft (89.0m), and have greater submerged displacement, 4,960 tons compared to 4,780 tons. Because of the large bow sonar the four 21in (533mm) torpedo tubes are mounted amidships and angled outwards.

Several boats of this class have been modified to carry the deep sea rescue vehicle (DSRV), a salvage and rescue submarine which sits on a special cradle on the after deck above the hatch. People can be transferred between the DSRV and the submarine when submerged. Three boats are to receive anechoic tile coatings in Fiscal Year 1988 and, if successful, more may be so equipped, in a similar manner to the latest Soviet and Royal Navy boats.

Production of this class ceased when USS *Richard B. Russell* (SSN 687) was launched in 1974. The planned life of each boat in the Sturgeon class is 30 years, thus SSN 687 will finally retire in 2004! One or more of the Sturgeon class are believed to have been fitted with contra-rotating propellers on the same shaft to reduce noise; although apparently successful, this has not been followed in any of the subsequent American SSN designs. Other modifications have included extensions to the after portion of the sail (SSN 679 and 687), while SSN 680 has a forward extension to her sail. Some also have various extra sonar fittings: SSN 687, for example, has two large sonar domes on the after deck.

USS *Narwhal* (SSN 671) was an experimental design based on the Sturgeon design and was built to test the S5G free-circulation reactor, which has no pumps and therefore is quieter than other United States reactors. This reactor depends upon forward movement to create a flow of cooling water. Although *Narwhal* retains this system and is still in front-line service, no further SSNs have been built with this system. However, the S5G led to the S8G natural-circulation reactor fitted to the Ohio-class SSBNs.

Right: USS Sea Devil *(SSN-664), one of 37 Sturgeon-class SSNs of the US Navy. Launched in 1967, she is expected to remain in service until 1997 at least, possibly longer.*

Right: USS Richard B Russell *(SSN-687), the last of the Sturgeon class SSNs to be built. Launched in 1971, she is fitted with four 21in (533mm) torpedo-tubes mounted amidships and angled outwards. The normal load is reported to be 15 Mk 48 dual-purpose torpedoes, four SUBROC anti-submarine missiles and four Sub-Harpoon anti-ship missiles.*

Origin: United States.
Type: Attack submarine, nuclear powered.
Displacement: Surfaced 4,460 tons; submerged 4,960 tons.
Dimensions: 302.2 x 31.75 x 26ft (92.1 x 9.7 x 7.9m).
Performance: Maximum speed (submerged) 30 knots.
Maximum diving depth: 1,312ft (400m).
Machinery: Nuclear: One pressurised water-cooled S5W2 reactor; two geared turbines; 20,000shp. Shafts: One.
Armament: Torpedo tubes: Four 21in (533mm). Missiles: Conventional torpedoes, Subroc and Mark 48 A/S torpedoes (23 total). Up to eight Tomahawk may be carried in lieu of other weapons.
Complement: 12 officers, 95 ratings.
Number in class: Built, 37.
Constructed: 1963 to 1974.
(Specifications apply to SSN 678 onwards; see text for earlier boats.)

Right: USS Richard B Russell. *Abaft the small sonar dome in the bow is a rectangular hatch housing the messenger buoy and above that on the top of the casing the blue circle marks the escape trunk. Below that on the hull is a Main Vent Valve.*

Trafalgar

The Royal Navy has followed a programme of steady improvement and refinement of its SSN designs since it became, with HMS *Dreadnought* in 1963, the second navy to operate SSNs. This boat was powered by an American S5W nuclear reactor and the general design was very similar to that of the US Navy's Skipjack class. However, like all subsequent Royal Navy submarines, it's foreplanes were mounted on the bow rather than on the sail. Dreadnought was taken out of service in 1981 and stricken in 1982.

Next came the five-boat Valiant class, the first of which was completed in July 1966. Although 19ft (5.8m) longer than the Dreadnought class, and with a somewhat larger crew complement (103 as opposed to 88), the Valiants are otherwise generally similar. HMS *Valiant* travelled 10,000 miles (16,093km) submerged from Singapore to Portsmouth in 28 days in 1967 in a demonstration of SSN capability. All five of the Valiant class have undergone long refits in the 1980s and will serve on until the mid-1990s.

The third class of British SSNs are the Swiftsures, the first of which joined the fleet in April 1973. These boats are 13ft (4m) shorter than the Valiant class, with a flat upper deck giving a different appearance to the humped-back of the earlier British SSNs. This new shape is evidence of a much greater internal volume, giving more space and better living conditions. The sail is lower than on earlier boats and the bow-mounted foreplanes are mounted so low on the hull that they are not visible when the submarine is on the surface. Previous British SSNs had six 21in (533mm) torpedo tubes, but in this class the number was reduced to five. Six boats were built between 1969 and 1979. They are very quiet and some, if not all, are coated with anechoic tiles made of an elastomeric material to reduce the submarine's acoustic signature, or, as it is euphemistically termed, "improve the noise hygiene".

The latest British SSNs to enter service are the Trafalgar class of seven boats. These are a development of the Swiftsure class and all are coated with a layer of rubber-compound anechoic tiles to reduce radiated and reflected noise. HMS *Trafalgar* the first of the class, has a standard propeller, but the remaining six boats have a shrouded pump-jet propulsion system, designed to reduce the noise signature yet further. This method of propulsion gives a higher top speed than a bladed propeller but with half the r.p.m.

The next class of British SSN will be the SSN 20 class, which will be powered by the Rolls-Royce PWR-2 reactor. The first order is due to be placed in 1990. SSN 20 will be a radically new design, with, among other features, a sail virtually in the bow.

Above: HMS Tireless *(S-117). The large sonar dome forward of the sail is the Type 2019* Paris *(Passive/Active Range and Intercept Sonar).*

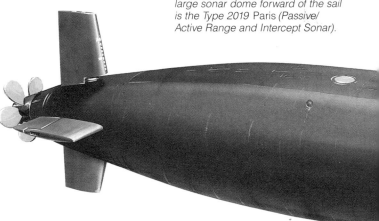

Origin: United Kingdom.
Type: Attack submarine, nuclear powered (SSN).
Displacement: Surfaced 4,700 tons; submerged 5,208 tons.
Dimensions: 280 x 32.25 x 27.06ft (85.38 x 9.83 x 8.25m).
Performance: Maximum speed (submerged) 30 knots.
Maximum diving depth: (Operating) 984ft (300m); (maximum) 1,640ft (500m).
Machinery: Nuclear: One PWR 1 pressurised water-cooled reactor, two English Electric turbines; 15,000shp. Diesel: One Paxman 400hp auxiliary diesel. Propeller: Shrouded pump-jet.
Armament: Torpedoe tubes: Five 21in (533mm). Missiles: 20 Mark 24 torpedoes or UGM-84B2 Sub-Harpoon.
Complement: 14 officers, 116 ratings.
Number in class: Built, 5; building, 2.
Constructed: 1979 and onwards to 1991.

Below: HMS Trafalgar (S-107), lead boat of the Royal Navy's latest class of SSN. The class is fitted with five 21in (533mm) torpedo tubes located just abaft the bow and is armed with MK 24 Tigerfish torpedoes and Sub-Harpoon missiles. Mines of various types can also be carried, including the Stonefish and Sea Urchin, shown here. Trafalgar is fitted with the standard propeller shown here, but the remaining boats in the class have British-designed and developed shrouded pump-jet propulsors for greater quietness.

Above: HMS Turbulent (S-110). British SSNs have developed progressively through Valiant and Swiftsure classes to today's Trafalgar class.

Agosta

The first of the Agosta class joined the French fleet in 1977 and has since been joined by three more, completing the French Navy's own order for this class. Four Agostas have also been built in Spain at the Bazan yard in Cartagena; they were launched between 1981 and 1984. One, *Sciroco* (S 72) collided with a destroyer in October 1985, but has been repaired. South Africa also wished to purchase two of this class, but were prevented from doing so by the international arms embargo. The two boats concerned were completed in France and sold to the Pakistan Navy in 1977/78; as built, they were identical with those delivered to the French Navy, but have since been modified to take the American Sub-Harpoon anti-

Origin: France.
Type: Attack submarine, diesel-electric (SSK).
Displacement: Surfaced 1,490 tons; submerged 1,740 tons.
Dimensions: 22.75 x 22.25 x 17.75ft (67.6 x 6.8 x 5.4m).
Performance: Maximum speed (submerged) 20.5 knots for 5 minutes, 17.5 knots for 60 minutes; (surfaced) 12 knots. Range 8,500nm (15,895km) at 9 knots (snorkel), 178nm (333km) at 3.5 knots (creep motor), 7,900nm (14,773km) (surface). Endurance 45 days.
Maximum diving depth: 984ft (300m).
Machinery: Diesel: Two SEMT-Pielstick 320-16 PA 4 185 diesel-generator sets (each 1,270bhp). Electric: One 3,500kw motor, plus one 23hp "creep" motor. Propeller: One five-bladed.
Armament: Torpedo tubes: Four 21.7in (550mm). Missiles: 20 L-5 Mod. 3 or F-17 torpedoes or SM-39 Exocet SSM.
Complement: 7 officers, 47 ratings.
Number in class: France, 4; Spain 4; Pakistan, 2.
Constructed: 1972 to 1976.

Below: The Pakistan submarine Hurmat (S-136), one of two Agosta-class submarines built by Dubigeon in France, 1976-78. These two boats were originally ordered by the Republic of South Africa Navy, but the order was cancelled due to the UN arms embargo. They are very quiet and highly automated boats, and the photograph shows the exceptionally smooth clean lines of the hull with the highly effective, five-bladed, slow revolution propeller.

Right: Agosta class diesel-electric patrol submarines are fitted with four bow torpedo tubes of 21.7in (550mm) diameter, capable of accepting either international standard 21in (533mm) or the older French 550mm torpedoes. Current outfit of the French boats consists of L5 Mod 3 free-running ASW torpedoes or F17 Mod 2 wire-guided anti-ship torpedoes. The French boats have been modified to fire SM-39 Exocet anti-ship cruise missiles, while the Pakistani boats can fire Sub-Harpoon. As far as is known, the Spanish boats can fire neither at present. Capacity is 20 torpedoes/missiles. Mines can be carried; three in place of each torpedo or missile.

ship missile. Egypt is also understood to have made enquiries about purchasing Agostas in the late-1970s, but no order was ever announced, four Chinese-built Romeos being purchased instead.

The Agosta class is somewhat larger than the previous Daphne class (1,043 tons submerged displacement) and is intended for distant-water operations, protecting the substantial remaining overseas interests of France. Great attention has been paid to silent operating. Only four torpedo tubes are fitted, but with 20 reloads and special devices for rapid reloading. The torpedo tubes are of 21.7in (550mm) calibre, which has been used by the French Navy for many years, but the international standard 21in (533mm) torpedoes can also be used. Normal weapon load is a combination of French designed and manufactured L-5 Mod. 3 or F-17 torpedoes or SM-39 Exocet anti-ship missiles.

The design incorporates a double-hull, with the space beteen the two being used for fuel, ballast and acoustic equipment. All equipment, such as sonar housings, which protrudes through the deck, is retractable to ensure a smooth waterflow at speed. One unusual feature is the fitting of a small 23hp electric motor for very quiet, low-speed cruising while on patrol.

If the French Navy maintains its announced intention to concentrate in future on nuclear-powered submarines the Agosta will have been the last of a very distinguished, effective and consistently interesting line of French-produced diesel-electric submarines.

Above: Agosta *(S-620) of the French Navy, which has four submarines of this class. There are four in the Spanish Navy and two with Pakistan.*

Kilo

Up to the Tango class, which entered service between 1972 and 1982, Soviet conventional submarine designers retained the traditional long, thin hull design, for some years after most other navies had adopted the shorter, fatter and much more efficient teardrop (''Albacore'') design. With the Kilo class, however, the Soviets, too, have produced a similar design of hull. They have also produced it at exactly the right time, as in the late-1970s many navies started looking around for successors to their 1950s vintage boats, such as Soviet Whiskey/Foxtrot type and the American Guppies.

Externally the Kilo class resemble modern Western conventional submarines (such as the Dutch Walrus and Japanese Yuushio) much more than do the earlier designs. However, there are still major differences. The Kilos are of double-hull construction, which gives greater survivability, although the row of free-flood holes may make for a ''noisier'' boat. The forward hydroplanes are fully retractable and are mounted just forward of the sail in the deck casing, an unusual position as most other modern submarines mount them either on the sail or much further forward on the bows. The after control surfaces are also unusual in that there is no vertical rudder above the stern, only a small tube-like tab, probably

Above: Kilo class diesel-electric submarine. About 8-10 serve with the Soviet Navy, but most of the 20 or so built have been for export.

Origin: USSR.
Type: Attack submarine, diesel-electric (SSK).
Displacement: Surfaced 2,500 tons; submerged 2,900 tons.
Dimensions: 239.5 x 32.5 x 21.3ft (73 x 9.9 x 6.5m).
Performance: Maximum speed (submerged) 25 knots; (surfaced) 16 knots.
Maximum diving depth: Not known.
Machinery: Diesel: Two; electric drive. Electric: One. Propeller: One six-bladed.
Armament: Torpedo tubes: Six 21in (533mm). Missiles: 12 torpedoes or 24 mines. Possible SAM system.
Complement: 60 total (approximately).
Number in class: Built, 18; building, 2 to 3 per year.
Constructed: 1980 onwards.

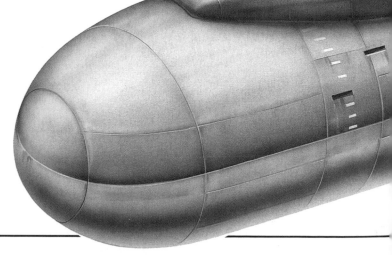

Below: The Kilo class has six 21in (533mm) bow torpedo tubes and stowage for an estimated 12 reloads. Two mines can be carried in place of each torpedo. So far as is known, these boats are not fitted to launch SS-N-15, nor have they the larger diameter 26in (650mm) tubes now being fitted in some Soviet submarines.

associated with a towed array. However, the Kilo is the first conventional Soviet design to have a single propeller.

Armament of the Kilo class is six bow-mounted 21in (533mm) torpedo tubes, with a total of 12 torpedoes. As far as is known the Kilos are not equipped for SS-N-15, nor do they have the new, larger 25.6in (650mm) tubes for SS-N-16. Some reports suggest that there may be a surface-to-air missile (SAM) launcher mounted in the sail.

The Kilo class is built at Komsomolsk-na-Amur in the Soviet Far East, and at Gorky and Leningrad in European Russia. The first boat was launched around 1980, the second in 1981 and since then production has been two to three boats per year. The Soviet Navy itself has about 12 Kilos in service and others have been ordered for export: Algeria (2), India (5), Romania (2), Poland (5). Of these orders, three of the Indian, two of the Polish and one of the Romanian have already been delivered. It is likely, too, that the Cuban and Libyan navies may also receive Kilos.

Tango

The Soviet Navy built some 75 long-range Foxtrot class diesel-electric submarines between 1957 and 1968, of which 15 were for export. These were intended primarily for anti-surface warfare against the much-feared US Navy carrier-centred task groups. However, in the late-1960s attention turned towards the ASW mission, especially in defence of the SSBN "bastions". The result was a mix of SSNs — the Victor class — and conventional SSKs — the Tangos.

The Tango class was first seen by Western observers at the Sebastopol Naval Review in July 1973. As far as is known production started in 1970 and continued until 1982, by which time some 22 had entered service with the Soviet Navy. It is of interest that no Tangos have ever been exported, even though the later Kilo SSK is being exported in some numbers.

Of identical length to the earlier Foxtrot class SSK, the Tango class has a much greater beam and much smoother lines and is sheathed in sonar-absorbent rubber compound. There is a noticeably raised bow section, almost certainly re-

Right: The Soviet Tango class diesel-electric patrol submarines represent the final development of a line of long-hull, twin propeller boats, which originated with the German World War Two Type XXI 'electroboot'. They are fitted with ten 21in (533mm) tubes, which can launch either conventional torpedoes or SS-N-15 missiles (similar to US SUBROC). It is probably significant that none have been exported, even to other Warsaw Pact navies.

quired to enable it to carry SS-N-15 missiles and the associated command-and-control facilities. The design incorporates two surprisingly old-fashioned ideas. The first, triple propellers, is similar to that of the Foxtrots, although at least one shaft is probably intended for very low speed/low noise-level "drifting". The second, four stern-mounted torpedo tubes, is a World War II concept. The Tangos are almost certainly the last to possess either. Photographs of the Tangos running on the surface give them a compact appearance, but this is misleading and they are, in fact, the largest and heaviest diesel-electric submarines to have been produced by any country for many years.

The balance of the large Soviet diesel-electric fleet consists of 45 Foxtrot and 48 Whiskey-class submarines. These elderly boats still serve a useful purpose in peacetime reconnaissance missions and would undoubtedly be used in secondary theatres in war; their combat value in major theatres such as the North Atlantic and against modern anti-submarine forces is, however, questionable.

Origin: USSR.
Type: Attack submarine, diesel-electric (SSK).
Displacement: Surfaced 3,100 tons; submerged 3,900 tons.
Dimensions: 300 x 29.52 x 22.96ft (91.5 x 9 x 7m).
Performance: Max speed (submerged) 16 kts; (surfaced) 20 kts.
Maximum diving depth: Not known.
Machinery: Diesel: Three diesel generators. Electric: Three electric motors. Propellers: Three five-bladed.
Armament: Torpedo tubes: Ten 21in (533mm) (6in bow, 4 aft). Missiles: Combination of torpedoes and SS-N-15 SSM.
Complement: 72.
Number in class: Built, 22.
Constructed: 1970 to 1982.

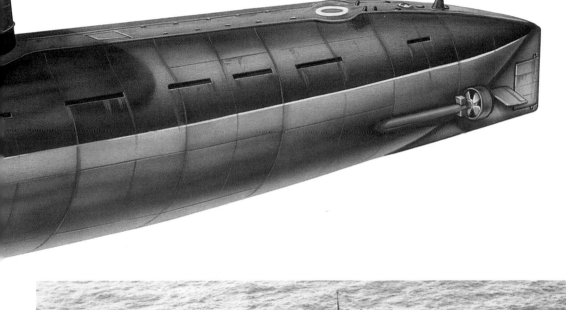

Below: A Tango class submarine at sea, showing most of her sail-mounted masts and antennas. The 'windows' on the forward edge of the sail are sonar panels. The large circles fore and aft indicate escape hatches and the round object forward is a communications buoy. The rise in the lines of the bow is thought to be needed to provide storage space for SS-N-15 missiles.

TR-1700

The West German firm of Thyssen Nordeseewerke started building submarines during World War II and constructed 30 Type VII-C U-boats between 1943 and 1945. They re-started submarine construction in the 1960s, building 15 Kobben class for the Royal Norwegian Navy (1962-67) and ten Type 206s for the Federal German Navy (1970-75).

The TR-1700 was designed by Thyssen Nordseewerke at Emden, having been developed from the slightly smaller TR-1400. Both were intended for export to meet the anticipated market as the large numbers of World War II designs (such as the ex-US Navy Guppies and Soviet Whiskies and Romeos) reached obsolescence in the 1980s. In the event only one country — Argentina — has ordered the design.

The TR-1700 has a submerged displacement of 2,364 tons making it among the larger submarines available for export. It is armed with six standard 21in (533mm) torpedo tubes, which normally fire SST-4 wire-guided torpedoes. There are 16 torpedo reloads and an automatic gear can reload a tube in just 50 seconds.

The original Argentine order for the TR-1400 was placed in November 1977 and thus well ahead of the South Atlantic conflict with the British in 1982. The Argentines already had two Type 209 submarines, which had been constructed in four sections in Germany and then shipped to Argentina where they were assembled. This experience was utilised in planning for the TR-1400, of which the first was to be constructed in Germany and the remainder in Argentina.

There have, however, been numerous changes to this plan. The order for TR-1400s was amended to the larger TR-1700s in February 1982 and two, instead of one, were built in the Thyssen Yards at Emden. Since the Falklands War, however,

Above: Santa Cruz (S-41), one of 5 units for Argentina. The first two were built in West Germany, the balance in Argentina.

Argentina has suffered from acute financial problems and the very expensive submarine programme has, not surprisingly, been the subject of intense government pressure. In 1986 Argentina obtained authority from the West German government to sell all of these submarines to a third party, and the boats being built in Argentina have been offered for

Origin: Federal Republic of Germany.
Type: Attack submarine, diesel-electric (SSK).
Displacement: Surfaced 2,150 tons; submerged 2,364 tons.
Dimensions: 216.5 x 23.95 x 21.32ft (66 x 7.3 x 6.5m).
Performance: Maximum speed (submerged) 25 knots, (snorkel) 13 knots; (surfaced) 15 knots. Range (submerged) 20nm (38km) at 25 knots, 50nm (94km) at 20 knots, 110nm (205km) at 15 knots, 460nm (860km) at 6 knots. Endurance 30 days.
Maximum diving depth: 984ft (300m).
Machinery: Diesel: Four MTU 16V652 MB80 1,100kw generator sets. Electric: One 6,600kw motor. Propeller: One five-bladed.
Armament: Torpedo tubes: Six 21in (533mm) torpedo tubes.
Missiles: 22 SST-4 wire-guided torpedoes.
Complement: 30.
Number in class: Built, 2; building, 3.
Constructed: 1980 onwards.

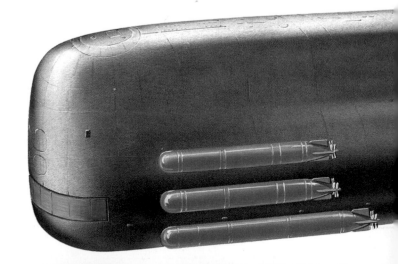

sale since 1984, but no known buyers are in the market. Boats 1 and 2 were delivered in December 1984 and November 1985 and are in service, but boats 3, 4 and 5 are still under construction at the Manuel Domecq Garcia Yard in Buenos Aires with the first not due for completion until 1991. As far as is known the sixth boat has not been laid down. Newspaper reports have suggested that the Argentine Navy is keen to build its own SSNs, but it is believed that President Alfonsin

Below: The TR-1700 has six bow 21in (533mm) torpedo tubes. Torpedoes currently in service with the Argentine Navy are the heavyweight SST-4, a development of the German Seal anti-ship torpedo, and the US Mk 37C ASW torpedo; both are wire-guided. It has been reported that Argentina wishes to sell these submarines.

Above: One of two Argentine TR-1700s under construction in the Thyssen yard at Emden in the early 1980s. The seven-bladed propeller is hidden, but the fine lines and cruciform control surfaces are clear.

has vetoed this very expensive project.

Six of the smaller Type 1000 are on order for Norway as the Ulla class. These are being delivered between February 1989 and April 1992. A similar design may be ordered for the Federal German Navy as the Type 211. Thyssen Nordeseewerke is also involved with the firm of Howaldtswerke-Deutsche Werft (HDW) in updating twelve German Type 206 submarines to Type 206A.

Type 209 (SSK-1500)

Probably the most successful series of submarine designs produced since World War II has been that emanating from the Ingenieur Kontor Lloyd (IKL) design bureau in West Germany. Many of their designs have been built in the West German submarine yards of Howaldtswerke-Deutsche Werft (Kiel) and Thyssen Nordseewerke (Emden), but, increasingly, technology transfer has enabled other countries to produce their own submarines.

The first in this series was the Type 205, of 450 tons displacement, six of which were built between 1961 and 1968 for the Federal German Navy. The first boats were built of a special non-magnetic steel which suffered severe corrosion; as a result U-1 and U-2 were totally rebuilt of a better steel, followed by U-9 to U-12 in a newer and more thoroughly tested non-magnetic steel. U-3 to U-8 have been stricken and U-1 was refitted in 1987 with a new experimental oxygen/hydrogen fuel-cell, closed-cycle, propulsion system. An improved version, designated Type 207, was built for Norway; of the 15 built, 11 remain, six of which are to be modernised and three transferred to Denmark.

The next design was the Type 206, of 498 tons displacement, with the greater battery power needed to meet the ever-growing demands of the electronic systems. Wire-guided torpedoes were also fitted. Between 1969 and 1974, 18 boats were built (U-13 to U-30) for the Federal German Navy. All are still in service in 1989 and 12 are being refitted to a new Type 206A standard.

The Type 209 is similar in shape and layout to the Type 205, but has increased dimensions, greater battery capacity and more powerful propulsion. Typical is the Argentine Salta

Origin: Federal Republic of Germany (and India).
Type: Attack submarine, diesel-electric.
Displacement: Surfaced 1,660 tons; submerged 1,860 tons.
Dimensions: 211.3 x 21.3 x 20.34ft (64.4 x 6.5 x 6.2m).
Performance: Maximum speed (submerged) 22.5 knots, (surfaced) 11 knots. Range (surface) 13,000nm (24,310 km) at 10 knots, (snorkel) 8,200nm (15,334km) at 8 knots. Endurance 50 days.
Maximum diving depth: Not known.
Machinery: Diesel: Four MTU 12V493 TY60 diesels (600hp each). Electric: Two Siemens motors. Propeller: One five-bladed.
Armament: Torpedo tubes: Eight 21in (533mm). Missiles: 14 torpedoes. Mines: Strap-on minelaying pods.
Complement: 8 officers, 28 ratings.
Number in class: See table.
Constructed: 1982 and onwards to 1991.
(Specifications apply to Indian SSK 1500; other Type 209 are different — see text.)

Above: The highly successful West German-designed Type 209 has eight swim-out tubes capable of firing any torpedo of 21in (533mm) diameter. Most of the navies which have purchased the Type 209 employ two complementary types of torpedo: generally, the long SST-4 anti-ship torpedo (shown here) and the short NT-37C ASW torpedo. The West German SUT dual-purpose torpedo is reported to be in service with the navies of Colombia, Ecuador and Indonesia. Chile and Peru use the Italian A.184 and Brazil the British Mk 24 Tigerfish. As far as is known none have been fitted to fire missiles.

class, with a surface displacement of 1,105 tons, a submerged displacement of 1,230 tons and an overall length of 183.4ft (55m). Eight 21in (533mm) torpedo tubes are fitted and the crew comprises 5 officers and 26 ratings. The hull is exceptionally smooth, with retractable hydroplanes mounted low on the bows, cruciform after control surfaces and a single propeller. Careful hull design and powerful motors result in an astonishing "burst" speed of 23 knots. Designed for patrols lasting 50 days, these boats are armed with eight 21in (533mm) torpedo tubes and have a full array of sensors.

There are minor differences between boats built for different countries. For example, the Chilean Type 209s have a sail 1.64ft (0.5m) higher to cope with the heavy seas off the coast of Chile.

Greece was the first country to place an order and, like several other countries, has followed this with a repeat order. The Type 209 has proved particularly popular in South America and with those navies joining the "submarine club" for the first time. The success story has been further helped by IKL's readiness for "technology transfer" enabling several countries to undertake submarine construction in their own yards for the first time, such as Turkey and Argentina.

The SSK-1500 was developed for the Indian Navy from the basic Type 209 and differs mainly in having a central bulkhead, which divides the pressure hull into two watertight sections; it is a slightly larger boat than other Type 209s. It also has the IKL-developed "crew-rescue sphere", which enables up to 40 men to escape simultaneously from considerable depths.

Type 471

Origin: Australia.
Type: Attack submarine, diesel-electric (SSK).
Displacement: Submerged 2,500 tons.
Dimensions: 246 x 24.6 x ?ft (75 x 7.5 x ?m).
Performance: Max speed (submerged) 21 kts; (surfaced) 12 kts.
Maximum diving depth: In excess of 984ft (300m).
Machinery: Diesel: Three Hedemora, 17-cylinder, 4-stroke, total 3.5MW. Electric: One Jeumont-Schneider DC motor. Propeller: One, seven-bladed, 14.4ft (4.4m) diameter.
Armament: Torpedo tubes: Six 21in (533mm). Missiles: 23 Sub-Harpoon SSM and Mark 48 torpedoes..
Complement: 46 officers and ratings.
Number in class: Building, 6 (option for two more).
Constructed: 1988 and onwards to 2000.

marine forces in Asian waters are those of China and India, both of which have nuclear-powered attack submarines, although obviously both American and Soviet submarines could also be in the area.

The NCSP is a highly-prestigious contract and has excited great interest among naval construction yards worldwide, as many of the world's conventional submarine fleets are becoming due for replacement in the next decade. Thus, tenders for the submarine design were received from virtually all the major Western diesel-electric submarine constructors, including Chantiers Dubigeon (France), Howaldtwerke/IKL (West Germany), Kockums (Sweden), RDM (Netherlands), Thyssen (West Germany) and Vickers (UK). After examination of the submissions Project Definition contracts were given to HDW/IKL and Kockums, with the latter eventually being declared the winners. The six submarines will be con-

For many years the Royal Australian Navy (RAN) borrowed both submarines and crews from the Royal Navy, but in the mid-1960s six British Oberon-class submarines were purchased and an RAN submarine arm established. These 2,417 ton Oxley-class boats have been very successful and have recently undergone a mid-life modernisation programme, which has included new electronics, sonars (including a clip-on, towed array) and fire-control systems. All are also being fitted for Sub-Harpoon.

In the late-1970s an A\$4,000 million New Construction Submarine Project (NCSP) was initiated to give the RAN a power-projection capability in areas of national strategic interest in the Pacific and Indian Oceans. There is no specific under-water threat to Australia and thus the RAN's NCSP mission was defined as being able to match qualitatively any vessel that it is liable to encounter in its defined operational area. Although no threat to the RAN, the most significant sub-

Below: A model of the Australian Type 471, eight of which are to be built by the Australian Submarine Corp, a consortium of Kockums (the Swedish designers), US CBI Industries and Australian firms.

structed in Australia by the Australian Submarine Consortium (ASC) at Port Adelaide. Similar competitive tenders were submitted for the combat system and a team made up of Rockwell International (United States) and Signaal (Netherlands) were eventually selected.

The Type 471 is an enlarged version of the Swedish Type A-17 Västergötland class. It is constructed of micro-alloy high-strength steel, developed in Sweden, which is as strong as HY8O, but is claimed to be easier to weld and fabricate. The submarine has two deck levels and internally is divided into two pressure-tight compartments.

There are six 21in (533mm) torpedo tubes, but there are no 15.75in (400mm) tubes as in the original Swedish Type A-17. A total of 23 weapons can be carried, which will comprise a selection of Sub-Harpoon missiles, Mark 48 torpedoes, mines, the actual combination depending upon the specific mission. Mention has also been made of tube-launched, land-attack cruise missiles (presumably the American Tomahawk) while the sail could also be utilised for vertical-launched missiles, if required.

Below: The design of the Type 471 is based upon that of the Swedish Västergötland, but incorporates developments to make it the quietest, most shock-resistant submarine in the world. Its armament will comprise 23 Harpoon SSM or Mk 48 torpedoes, using six bow-mounted 21in (533mm) launch tubes.

Upholder

HMS *Onyx,* the final boat of the Oberon class, entered service with the Royal Navy in 1967 and it was intended that the Oberons should be the last class of diesel-electric submarines. In the intervening years, however, the Royal Navy has come to accept that, while the nuclear-powered submarine has many advantages, there is still a need for the conventional type as well. Accordingly, the decision was made in 1983 to procure the new Upholder class.

The Upholder is based on the Vickers Type 2400 design, which was a private venture undertaking offered to several

Origin: United Kingdom.
Type: Attack submarine, diesel-electric (SSK).
Displacement: Surfaced 2,185 tons; submerged 2,400 tons.
Dimensions: 230.5 x 24.9 x 18.0ft (70.26 x 7.6 x 5.5m).
Performance: Maximum speed (submerged) 20 knots; (surfaced) 12 knots. Range 10,000nm (18,700km) plus. Endurance 49 days; typical patrol of 8 knots transit, 28 days in area.
Maximum diving depth: 820+ft (250+m).
Machinery: Diesel: Two Paxman-Valenta, 16 RPA 200SZ, 16-cylinder diesel generators, 2,035hp each. Electric: Two GEC, 2,500kw alternators. Propeller: One, seven-bladed.
Armament: Torpedo tubes: Six 21in (533mm). Missiles: 18 Mark 24 or Spearfish torpedoes, or Sub-Harpoon SSM.
Complement: 7 officers, 37 ratings.
Number in class: Built, 2; building, 2 (see text).
Constructed: 1986 and onwards to 1992.

Below: HMS Upholder *(S-40) at the VSEL Yard at Barrow-in-Furness, England. Four of this class are on order and eight more may follow. The fifth and later boats may be stretched to accomodate more powerful propulsion units and to achieve greater endurance.*

Above: The Upholders are capable of launching the complete range of Royal Navy submarine weapons through their six 21in (533mm) bow tubes. Initially the Mk 24 Tigerfish will be carried, but this will be replaced in due course by the Spearfish; both are dual-purpose, ie, they can be used against either surface or submerged targets. The Upholder class is also fitted to launch Sub-Harpoon missiles. Finally, Stonefish mines can be carried in place of torpedoes.

overseas navies. The single-hull form is based closely upon that of the British SSNs and has a high beam-to-length ratio, with a pressure-hull constructed of NQ-1 steel (equivalent to HY-80). Internally, the hull is subdivided by two main bulkheads, with the two forward watertight compartments having two deck levels and the after (machinery) space a single deck. The outer hull is coated in elastomeric tiles, which are intended to muffle self-noise and to reduce sonar returns, thus contributing to the exceptional "quietness" of the design. As with the Oberons, the skin of the sail is glass-reinforced plastic (GRP) to conserve weight.

The Upholder class has large battery capacity which gives them a high underwater speed and endurance, but they still need to snorkel, which can be done at speeds of up to 19 knots. They are intended to be very reliable and are designed to operate for 15,000 hours (equivalent to seven years in commission) between major refits. As with other modern SSK designs, a noteworthy economy in manpower is achieved by the greatly increased use of automation. The Upholder class requires a crew of 7 officers and 37 ratings compared with 6 officers and 62 ratings for the Oberon class.

There are six bow-mounted 21in (533mm) torpedo tubes in two banks; two in the upper bank and four below. A further 12 reloads are carried for a total of 18. This can be a mix of Tigerfish torpedoes, Sub-Harpoon ASMs and Stonefish mines, and, in the future, Spearfish torpedoes.

Currently four Upholder class are on order: HMS *Upholder* was commissioned in 1988 and the remaining three units will join the fleet in 1991, 1992 and 1993, respectively. However, it is believed that the Royal Navy's eventual target is ten boats, with the fifth onwards being of a stretched design of 3,000 tons (surfaced), capable of greater endurance.

Västergötland

Sweden has built her own submarines since 1904, specially designed to cope with Baltic conditions. The firm of Kockums built their first submarine in 1914 and became the sole Swedish submarine design authority in 1950 (there is no naval design office). The oldest Swedish submarines currently in service are the four remaining boats of the Dräken (Type A-11) class. Six were built in the early-1960s, but these 770 tons displacement boats are now elderly and are being replaced in 1989-90.

The five submarines of the Sjöormen (Type A-11B) class joined the fleet between 1967 and 1969. The 1,400 tons displacement design was based, like so many others, upon lessons learned from the US Navy's revolutionary "Albacore" hull. The Swedish design incorporated forward hydroplanes mounted on a common shaft on the large sail, although it was one of the few to adopt the Albacore indexed (X-shaped) cruciform after control surfaces. Endurance is estimated at some three weeks. The 23-man crew is a considerable reduction on the 44 required by the previous Dräken class.

Next came the three-strong Näcken (Type A-14) class, launched 1978-79. Displacing 1,125 tons these boats are capable of operating at depths of up to 984ft (300m) — with a crush depth of 1,640ft (500m) which suggests that they are expected to operate outside the Baltic in the trenches of the Skaggerak. Based on the Sjöormen design, the Näcken is slightly smaller and great attention has been paid to quietness and control at very slow speeds. Yet further automation reduced the crew to 19. These boats also introduced the unusual mixed armament of six 21in (533mm) and two 15.75in (400mm) torpedo tubes. The larger torpedo is the Type 613, a 23ft (7.025m) long, wire-guided/homing torpedo, with a wakeless hydrogen peroxide engine and a range of 32,800 yards (30,000m). The

Origin: Sweden.
Type: Attack submarine, diesel-electric (SSK).
Displacement: Surfaced 1,070 tons; submerged 1,140 tons.
Dimensions: 159.1 x 19.88 x 20.0ft (48.5 x 6.06 x 6.10m).
Performance: Maximum speed (submerged) 20 knots; (surfaced) 10 knots.
Maximum diving depth: In excess of 984ft (300m).
Machinery: Diesel: Two Hedemora V12A/15-Ub, each 1,080hp. Electric: Two Jeumont-Schneider 760kw generators, one ASEA electric motor, 1,800shp. Propeller: One five-bladed.
Armament: Torpedo tubes: Six 21in (533mm), four 15.75in (400mm). Missiles: 12 Type 613 21in (533mm) torpedoes; six Type 422 or Type 431 15.75in (400m) torpedoes.
Complement: 5 officers, 12 ratings.
Number in class: Built, 3; building, 1.
Constructed: 1983 to 1989.

smaller, 15.75in (400mm), torpedo is the Type 423, a wire-guided/acoustic homing ASW torpedo, 8.53ft (2.60mm) long. Following a series of embarrassing Swedish experiences with underwater intruders into her territorial waters a special version of the Type 423 has been developed with a reduced charge for use against such incursions.

Continuing this line of development the four-strong Västergötland (Type A-17) class was launched between 1986 and 1989. Like all Swedish submarines since the Dräken class these are assembled at the Kockums Yard in Malmö. Kockums also build the centre section, while the bow and stern sections are fabricated by Karlskrona. The torpedo tubes are arranged with the six larger 21in (533mm) tubes above the four shorter 15.75 (400mm) tubes, but with separate reload magazine compartments. Consideration is being given to these boats being fitted with four vertical launch tubes in the sail for RBS-17 anti-ship missiles. This missile is a version of the Saab RBS-15 surface-skimmer, powered by a solid fuel booster rocket and a turbojet sustainer. It has terminal-homing guidance.

The X-configuration rudders have no mechanical connections with each other, being individually controlled from a computerised steering control system developed by Saab-Scania. One particular advantage of this ''X'' arrangement is that none of the rudders extend beyond the maximum diameter of the hull, thus simplifying both mooring and, more importantly, lying on the seabed.

In a very significant development, Kockums rebuilt the *Näcken* in 1987/88 to take an extra section incorporating a Stirling air-independent propulsion system, which includes the Stirling generators, the liquid-oxygen (LOX) supplies and control systems. This submarine is not a laboratory test-bed, but is a fully operational submarine.

Left: Västergötland *shows her torpedo tubes: six 21in (533m) above and four 15.7in(400mm) below. There is some talk of fitting four vertical launch tubes in the sail for the RBS-17 anti-ship missile, a development of the RBS-15 sea-skimming weapon.*

Below: Västergötland *is the latest in a long line of Swedish submarine designs stretching back to the early 1900s. Developed for Swedish (primarily Baltic) conditions, the design has nevertheless formed a very satisfactory basis for the Australian Type 471 (see earlier) for use in the Pacific and Indian Oceans. The indexed, cruciform after control surfaces are operated and controlled by computer.*

Yuushio

The Imperial Japanese Navy had one of the world's major submarine fleets during World War II and built some unusual types. Their largest submarines, the 6,560 tons (submerged) I-400 (STo) class, were the biggest to be built by any navy prior to the development of nuclear propulsion. In the early-1950s the Japanese Maritime Self-Defense Force (JMSDF), like many other United States allies, received surplus US Navy submarines of World War II vintage, but with post-war streamlining and equipment updates.

As the Japanese economy gained strength, the JMSDF looked towards restoring indigenous shipbuilding capability and the first Japanese post-war submarine, the *Oyashio* (1,420 tons submerged), appeared in 1959. This design was very conventional and was followed by the improved four-boat Hayashio class in 1961-62. Yet further improvement of the basic design followed with the Ooshio class (1,650 tons standard), these being among the last submarines to be produced with stern torpedo tubes.

The next class, Uzushio, was, like many other contemporary Western designs, based on that of the US Navy's *Barbel,* with an *Albacore*-type teardrop hull for faster and quieter underwater performance. Of 2,430 tons (submerged) displacement, the hull was built of very high-quality steel to give a diving depth of 650ft (198m). Seven boats were built beteen 1969 and 1977 and the name ship of the class, *Uzushio,* was stricken in 1987 followed by *Makishio* in 1988, each after only 16 years service. Presumably the remaining five will be similarly stricken at the 16-year point.

The latest class to enter service is the Yuushio class. There are ten boats in service, the eleventh and final boat is due to enter service in December 1990. The Yuushio class is basically an all-round improvement on the Uzushio class, capable of slightly higher speeds. Both the Uzushio class and the

Above: The Japanese submarine Mochishio (SS-574), one of the eleven-strong Yuushio class of SSK. Displacing some 3,800tons submerged, these vessels are among the most effective diesel-electric submarines in service in any navy.

Above: The Japanese Yuushio class diesel-electric patrol submarines are fitted with six 21in (533mm) torpedo tubes, which are in two banks of three below the sail. They are angled outwards in the manner of US SSNs, in order to leave the bow clear for the large ZQQ-4 sonar array. The Japanese Maritime Self-Defence Force (JMSDF) currently uses the US Mk 48 heavyweight and short Mk 37C ASW torpedoes. These will eventually be replaced by a new high-performance torpedo of indigenous design, designated GRX-2. In World War II Japanese torpedoes were among the best in use in any navy so this new type should also have a very high combat effectiveness.

Origin: Japan.
Type: Attack submarine, diesel-electric (SSK).
Displacement: Surfaced 2,200 tons.
Dimensions: 249.25 x 32.5 x 24.58ft (76.2 x 9.9 x 7.5m).
Performance: Max speed (submerged) 20 kts; (surfaced) 12 kts.
Maximum diving depth: 3,280ft (1,000m).
Machinery: Diesel: Two Mitsubishi/MAN V8/V24-30 AMTL Kawasaki diesel generator sets (each 1,700hp). Electric: One Fuji electric motor, 7,220hp. Propeller: One, seven-bladed.
Armament: Torpedo tubes: Six 21in (533mm) torpedo tubes. Missiles: 12 to 15 Mark 48 wire-guided or Mark 37C ASW torpedoes.
Complement: 10 officers, 70 ratings.
Number in class: Built, 11.
Constructed: 1976 to 1989.

Yuushio class submarines have their torpedo tubes mounted amidships, a feature they share with US Navy SSNs, which frees the bow area for a large sonar array. The torpedo tubes are canted outwards at an angle of 10°.

The Uzushio class is built of NS-63 high-tensile steel, but the Yuushios are constructed of NS-90, increasing permitted diving depth from 656ft (200m) to 984ft (300m). These Japanese boats are very sophisticated, as would be expected from such a technologically-advanced nation, and would seem to be equivalent to SSNs in most features except one — the crucial one of underwater endurance. This will undoubtedly push the JMSDF towards seeking a solution to the problem of freeing the diesel-electric submarine from the necessity to come up to "breathe" at regular intervals.

The next class of submarines will be an improved version of the Yuushio class, slightly longer and with surface displacement increased from 2,250 tons to 2,400 tons. The first boat is due to be launched in 1990 and to enter service with the JMSDF in 1991.

Zeeleeuw

The Dutch have a well-deserved reputation for innovative submarine design. It was a Dutch naval officer who invented the "schnorkel" tube in the mid-1930s and one of the most remarkable post-war submarine designs was the four boat, triple-hulled Dolfijn class, completed in the years 1962 to 1966. Of 1,830 tons submerged displacement, three of these boats will remain in service until the early-1990s.

These were followed in 1970-71 by the Zwaardvis class. These two boats (2,640 tons displacement) were among the largest conventional submarines in service for some years. Their design was based upon that of the US Navy's *Barbel*, with a similar *Albacore* hull, giving considerable internal depth and a roomy two-deck interior. A single five-bladed propeller is mounted abaft the cruciform control surfaces, powered by a 3,800kw electric motor.

Following on from the Zwaardvis class is the six-boat Zeeleeuw class. Unfortunately, the first boat of this class, *Walrus*, was damaged by fire in 1986 and it was thought that she would have to be scrapped. However, she is now being rebuilt, adding over 30 per cent to her total cost and will not now join the fleet until 1990. *Zeeleeuw* has thus become the first to enter service and the class has been named after her, rather than after the unfortunate *Walrus*.

The Zeeleeuw class has a displacement of 2,800 tons, making them among the largest of contemporary diesel-electric submarines. They are constructed of French "Marel" high-tension steel, which gives a 50 per cent increase in diving depth over the Zwaardvis class. Much greater use of automation has enabled the crew to be reduced from 8 officers and 59 ratings in the Zwaardvis to 7 officers and 43 ratings in the Zeeleeuw class, a substantial saving in manpower and training costs.

The Netherlands government sold two modified versions of the Zwaardvis class to the navy of the Republic of China (Taiwan). Although this caused some political problems with the People's Republic of China, the original order for two boats was honoured, both being built by Wilton-Fijenoord. Taiwan planned to build a further four boats herself, but problems involved in setting up her own construction facilities for such large and sophisticated submarines led to a request to the Dutch to build two more. However, various factors, not least of which was political pressure from Peking, prevented Taiwanese requests being met. The boats actually delivered, the Hai Lung or Sea Dragon class, have a submerged displacement of 2,600 tons, and incorporate a high degree of automation and computerisation.

Above: This picture shows one of the Zeeleeuw class boats under construction. A notable innovation of this class is the adoption of X-planes in the place of conventional cruciform tail surfaces. X-planes give finer control of depth and bearing and permit 'bottoming'. The forward hydroplanes are high on the front of sail.

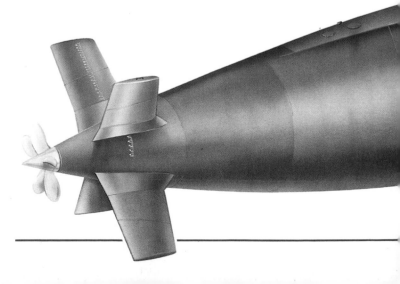

Origin: The Netherlands.
Type: Attack submarine, diesel-electric (SSK).
Displacement: Surfaced 2,450 tons; submerged 2,800 tons.
Dimensions: 222.2 x 27.6 x 23ft (67.73 x 8.4 x 7m).
Performance: Maximum speed (submerged) 21 knots; (surfaced) 12 knots. Range (snorkel) 10,000nm (18,700km) at 9 knots.
Maximum diving depth: 984ft (300m).
Machinery: Diesel: Three SEMT-Pielstick 12PA4V 200. Electric: One Holec 5,430shp motor. Propeller: One, five-bladed.
Armament: Torpedo tubes: Four 21in (533mm). Missiles: 20 Sub-Harpoon SSM or Mark 48 or NT.37C/D/E torpedoes.
Complement: 7 officers, 43 ratings.
Number in class: Built, 1; building, 4 (+1).

Above: Zeeleeuw being launched from the RDM shipyard. This class was originally named after Walrus, the first boat under construction. This vessel was severely damaged by a fire during construction and the class was renamed after the second vessel, Zeeleeuw.

Below: The Zeeleeuw class has four 21in (533mm) bow torpedo tubes which use the 'water slug' method of launching weapons. Torpedoes carried can be the US Mk 48 dual-purpose torpedo or the NT-37 short anti-submarine torpedo. These boats are also fitted with fire control equipment for the Sub-Harpoon anti-ship missile. There is stowage space for up to 16 reloads.

India

Several navies have developed deep-sea rescue vehicles (DSRV), following the US Navy lead after the loss of USS *Thresher* (SSN 593) on April 10, 1963. This led the US Navy to develop *Mystic* (DSRV 1) and *Avalon* (DSRV 2), which were completed 1971-72 and remain in service today. These US Navy DSRVs are air-mobile in Lockheed C-141 Starlifter transport aircraft and can then be delivered to the scene of the accident by sitting on a special mounting on another submarine or by a special surface rescue ship of the Pidgeon (ASR 21) class. The DSRVs can operate at a maximum depth of 4,920ft (1,500m) and can bring up to 24 men to the surface at one time.

The Soviet Navy has a large submarine fleet and has a much worse accident record than do any of the Western navies. Since 1980 one Charlie class SSGN, one Yankee class SSBN and the Mike class SSN are known to have sunk, while numerous others have had accidents which involved damage and loss of life, but without actual loss of the submarine at sea. Clearly, therefore, the Soviet Navy needs its own rescue capability, but chose a somewhat different approach to that of the United States. The basis of the Soviet system is the India-class submarine, of which two are known to exist, one with the Northern Fleet and the other with the Pacific Fleet. The two Indias are purpose-built for the role and are, in fact, not only the largest diesel-electric submarines in service, but are also among the largest conventional submarines ever built, with a length of 348ft (106m) and a submerged displacement of 4,800 tons.

Of conventional double-hull construction, the India design appears to have been based upon that of the Foxtrot. The major feature is the large after deck with two docking wells to accommodate two submersibles. The hull and after deck have a generous number of free-flood holes. Uniquely among Soviet diesel-electric submarines the forward hydroplanes are mounted on the sail, rather than low down on the bow.

Right: India class rescue submarine, with its two rescue submersibles in place. Built in the late 1970s, there are just two Indias; one is with the Pacific Fleet, the other with the Northern Fleet.

Origin: USSR.
Type: Rescue/salvage.
Displacement: Surfaced 3,900 tons; submerged 4,800 tons.
Dimensions: 348 x 33 x ?ft (106 x 10 x ?m).
Performance: Max speed (submerged) 15 kts; (surfaced) 15 kts.
Maximum diving depth: Not known.
Machinery: Diesel: Two. Electric: Two. Propellers: Two.
Armament: Probably none.
Complement: Not known.
Number in class: Built, 2.
Constructed: 1978 to 1979.

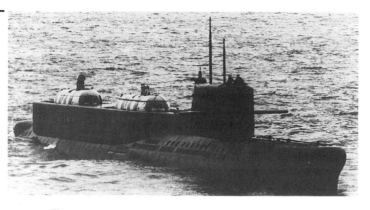

The Indias are designed to travel on the surface to the area of the accident and then submerge, prior to deploying the submersibles. As far as is known the Indias have no weapon carrying capability.

Two types of submersible have been seen on the Indias. Both are painted white, with red/orange stripes, presumably to indicate their rescue status. Both consist of a cylindrical centre-section with a bulbous bow and a pointed stern, with a single propeller. The main differences between the two types are that the first is 37ft (11.3m) long and has two shrouded and rotatable propellers on either side of its after section. The second is 40ft (12.1m) long and is powered by a single shrouded propeller. Both submersibles have a small conning-tower on the upper deck and are also fitted with a large circular hatch in their undersides to enable them to mate with similar fittings in both the crippled submarine and in the docking wells of the India class. It would appear that these Soviet DSRVs are constructed of two, interlinked titanium spheres within the streamlined outer casing.

Left: The submarines of the India class are thought to be unarmed, the bow-form being too fine to accommodate torpedo tubes. The two submersibles carried are for rescue purposes only: their construction is probably based on two titanium pressure spheres. There is a small hatch atop the outer casing, and a larger circular mating hatch beneath to provide access to and from the submarine.

Left: The two submersibles have their own separate wells. They are fitted with caterpiller tracks to enable them to move along the ocean-floor. They are also fitted with collars to enable them to mate with special rescue hatches built into the upper casing of all Soviet submarine types.

Ballistic Missiles

SLBMs have transformed submarines into major strategic weapons systems, which threaten the enemy's homeland with devastating nuclear retaliation. SSBNs are sea-mobile, missile launching pads and, as such, transport the SLBMs and provide them with protection from the elements and hostile action up to the moment of launch. As part of this function the submarine provides the other sub-systems with electrical, hydraulic and pneumatic power, together with temperature and environmental control, and overall systems monitoring.

Each missile is housed in its own launch tube. To launch the missile the outer hatch is opened exposing the tube end-cap. On the order to fire the missile is ejected with some force, usually by an explosive charge, rupturing the end-cap as it leaves the tube. When approximately 90ft (27.43m) clear of the tube the first-stage motor ignites and the missile is propelled up to the surface and on, up into the atmosphere, where the expended first stage separates and falls away. The second-stage motor then ignites and propels the missile on its way, followed — in the case of the latest SLBMs such as Trident, SS-N-23 and M-4 — by ignition of the third-stage motor to push the missile into a high arc.

Early SLBMs had one re-entry vehicle (RV) each. However, technological advances then made it possible to place several warheads, known as multiple re-entry vehicles (MRV), on each missile; these were all aimed at the same target. The next refinement was multiple independently-targettable re-entry vehicles (MIRVs), which, as their name implies, could be directed at different targets by being released from the ''bus'' at different points. Although more accurate than MRVs, these MIRVs are still not as accurate as those fired from land-based ICBMs, and thus can only be used to attack area targets. In future, however, SLBMs may be fitted with manoeuvrable re-entry vehicles (MaRV), which can be steered onto their targets with great precision. This would, of course, give the SLBMs, for the first time, a ''first-strike'' capability.

US Navy Trident I (C-4) missiles have an ''aerospike'', which extends after launch, creating the same aerodynamic effect as a sharp, slender nose; this reduces drag by some 50 per cent, thus enhancing range. Allied to a third-stage motor and improved fuel, this gives the missile a full payload (eight MIRVs) range of 4,230nm (7,833km), compared to 2,500nm (4,630km) for Poseidon (C-3); range can be increased by reducing the RV payload. To overcome inherent inaccuracies in the submarine inertial navigation system (SINS) of SSBNs,

US fleet ballistic missiles

Soviet fleet ballistic missiles

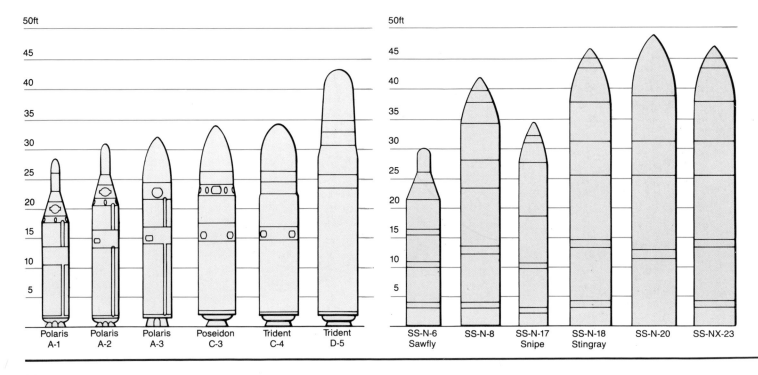

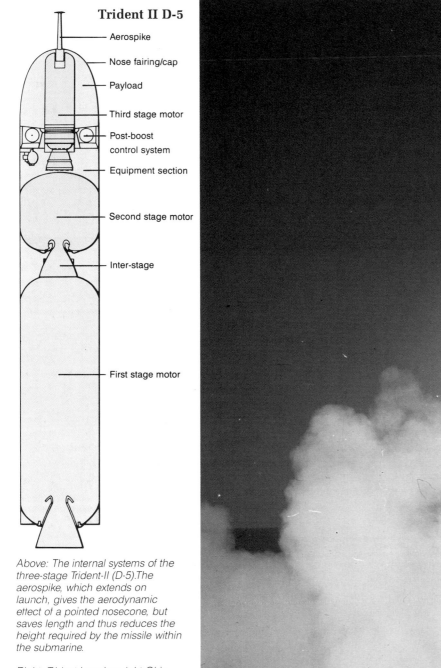

Trident II D-5

- Aerospike
- Nose fairing/cap
- Payload
- Third stage motor
- Post-boost control system
- Equipment section
- Second stage motor
- Inter-stage
- First stage motor

Above: The internal systems of the three-stage Trident-II (D-5).The aerospike, which extends on launch, gives the aerodynamic effect of a pointed nosecone, but saves length and thus reduces the height required by the missile within the submarine.

Right: Trident-I equips eight Ohio (24 missiles) and twelve Lafayette/Franklin (16 missiles) class ballistic missile submarines.

the Mark 5 inertial navigation system in the Trident I (C-4) missile incorporates stellar updating — a sensor takes a star sight during the post-boost phase, which enables it to correct the flight path. The eight Mark 4 RVs (W-76 warheads, 100kT yield), have a reported accuracy circular error probable (CEP) of 0.25nm (457m), which may reduce to 0.12nm (229m) with future developments.

The Trident II (D-5) missile has even greater payload and accuracy. It is longer and has slightly increased diameter than Trident I (C-4); although capable of carrying 14 RVs it is limited by the SALT II agreements to ten. The Mark 5 RV has a yield of 475kT and a cep of 0.19nm (122m); according to the Pentagon it is designed to take different warheads "tailored to the target assignment". The Trident II (D-5) is scheduled to equip 20 US Navy Ohio-class SSBNs and the four new British SSBNs. Each United States SSBN will have 24 missiles, each with ten RVs, i.e. a total war load of 240 RVs.

The Soviet Navy's two latest SLBMs are SS-N-20 on the Typhoon class and SS-N-23 on the Delta IV. SS-N-20 is a three-stage solid-fuel missile with a range of 4,800nm (8,890km), carrying six to nine RVs. On October 21, 1982 the first Typhoon-class SSBN conducted a simultaneous launch of four SS-N-20s. Cep is 0.35nm (640m). The second new missile, SS-N-23, is a three-stage weapon with seven MIRVs and a range of some 5,000nm. It has greater throw-weight and accuracy than the SS-N-18 fitted to the Delta III SSBNs, but, surprisingly, it is liquid-fuelled. All these missiles can reach any target in the United States, even if launched from the SSBN in its home port or within territorial waters.

The current British SLBM is Polaris A-3TK. Bought from the United States in the 1960s, these missiles were remotored in the early-1980s, and have recently been fitted with an entirely new front-end, designated Chevaline. Each missile is reported to carry six MRVs with a nominal yield of 150kT each. The Royal Navy's new Vanguard-class SSBNs will carry 16 Trident II (D-5) missiles, each with eight British designed

Above: The Polaris SLBM has long since been replaced in the US Navy by Poseidon and Trident. It is now only used, in the version seen here, by the British. The missile is US-made, but warheads and guidance systems are of British design and manufacture. The massively expensive Chevaline programme will maintain the deterrence value of British Polaris missiles until Trident enters service on the Vanguard class of SSBN in the 1990s.

Left: A Trident-I missile canister is lowered into the hull of an Ohio class SSBN. There are two docking facilities such is this: one at Bangor, Washington, the other at King's Bay, Georgia. By agreement with the USSR the covered portion is shorter than the submarine to enable satellite verification that a submarine is using the facility.

and constructed MIRVs.

The latest French SLBM is the M-4, a three-stage missile carrying six 150kT MIRVs, installed in *L'Inflexible* and being retro-fitted to earlier SSBNs (currently fitted with M-20) except the oldest, *Le Redoutable.* The launch interval between missiles is shorter for the M-4 than for the M-20 and the launch depth is greater. The M-4 has six TN-70 MIRVs with a footprint of 81x189nm (150x350km) at a range of 2,160nm. A new version, the M-45, has a range of 2,700nm (5,000km). A totally new missile, the M-5, is being developed for the next generation of French SLBM, which will carry eight to twelve new (TN-75) MIRVs to a range of 3,240nm (6,000km).

Those SSBNs held by the People's Republic of China, of which at least two are in service, are armed with 12 CSS-N-3 SLBMs. This missile carries one RV to a range of 1,500nm (2,795km). Newer, MIRVed, and longer-range missiles are under development.

Cruise Missiles

In the late-1940s virtually every operational submarine had its gun removed and for many years the only weapons for use against surface ships and other submarines were torpedoes. From the early-1950s, however, a variety of guided-missile systems have been fitted to submarines, giving them a much-enhanced capability to attack — with either nuclear or conventional warheads — distant surface warships or land targets far beyond the shoreline. At first, such missiles were confined to highly-specalised cruise-missile submarines but now their use is much more general.

Submarine-launched cruise missiles (SLCM) have been deployed by the Soviet Navy since the 1960s using specialised boats to carry them. Current types are the Juliett-class diesel-electric cruise-missile submarines (SSG) and the nuclear-powered boats (SSGN) (Echo, Charlie and Oscar classes) which carry SLCM mounted in bins, either amidships or in the bows. The missiles (SS-N-3, -7, -9, and -19) can be launched from underwater and have ranges up to 600-miles (966km). Their most probable role is in attacking NATO task groups in the North Atlantic, especially those formed around attack aircraft carriers. The most recent design, the SS-N-24, is being tested in a specially-converted Yankee-class submarine (formerly an SSBN); this cruise missile has a reported range of 2,200nm.

Surprisingly, the People's Republic of China has recently developed an anti-ship, surface-launched cruise missile, the C-801 Yinji. Six of these missiles are mounted in individual tubes on the upper casing of the Project E5SG diesel-electric submarine. Range of the Yinji is some 40nm (75km).

The US Navy took a different approach and to avoid developing specialised submarines decided to produce weapons launched from standard 21in (533mm) torpedo tubes. This was successfully applied to the Sub-Harpoon anti-ship missile and the Tomahawk which exists in two versions, one for anti-ship missions (T-ASM) and the other for land attack (T-LAM). After vast expenditure on making the Tomahawk suitable for launching from torpedo tubes it has been realised that for every Tomahawk missile carried one less valuable torpedo can go to sea; it has, therefore, been decided to fit the Tomahawk in vertically-mounted tubes in-

Below: Sub-Harpoon's role is to deliver a 500lb (230kg) penetration/blast warhead over ranges of up to 60nm against surface ships. It is propelled out of the sea and into the air by a solid rocket booster then the turbojet sustainer takes over. After reaching an altitude of 5,000ft (1,500m) the missile dives to low level to cruise at high subsonic speed, homing on to the target.

Sub-Harpoon launch profile

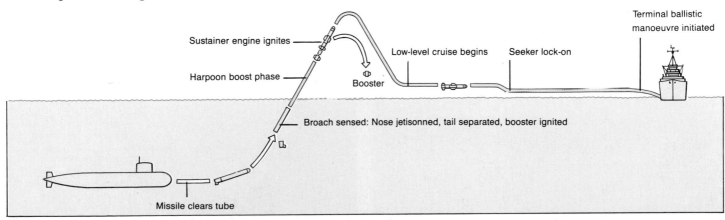

Terminal ballistic manoeuvre initiated

Sustainer engine ignites

Low-level cruise begins   Seeker lock-on

Harpoon boost phase

Booster

Broach sensed: Nose jetisonned, tail separated, booster ignited

Missile clears tube

side the upper casing between the bow sonar and the forward end of the pressure hull. This is a significant capability enhancement at little cost, but it is now irrelevant as to whether the missile can fit a torpedo tube or not, and thus much research and development money and effort has been wasted on the size-reduction programme.

Sub-Harpoon can attack ships out to 60 miles (97km) and the T-ASM to 250 miles (400km), while the T-LAM has a range of 1,367 miles (2,200km), and has both conventional and nuclear warheads. The main problem with T-LAM is that to exploit its capabilities fully it needs external target information and a system known as Outlaw Shark is being deployed to achieve this. The deployment of Tomahawk in this role has, however, increased the need for two-way communications with submarines, a notoriously difficult problem. The Soviet Navy has also now produced a torpedo-tube launched cruise missile, SS-N-21, with a range of some 1,600nm (2,992km).

The only other submarine-launched anti-ship missile is

Below: A submarine-launched Tomahawk land-attack missile arrives precisely on target on San Clemente Island, off the Californian coast, after a flight of some 400nm. Planned procurement of all versions of Tomahawk is 3,994 missiles with 2,600 potentional launchers: submarines, surface ships and aircraft. In launch configuration the missile weighs 3,400lb (1,542kg), with the launch canister used in submarines adding another 604lb (274kg) to this weight.

Below: The explosion as the Tomahawk destroys the aircraft in its hardened pen. The conventional 'bullpup' warhead weighs some 1,000lb (454kg). The other type of warhead is nuclear and this presents a defender with a dilemma as it is almost impossible to verify whether an incoming cruise missile is armed with a conventional or nuclear warhead. The danger is that he may take the worst case, assume it must be nuclear and act accordingly.

the French SM39 Exocet, a new version of the very successful surface-launched missile which achieved such a reputation in the 1982 South Atlantic conflict. Launched from a standard 21in (533mm) torpedo tube the SM39 has a range of over 27nm (50km). The system became operational in 1985 on board the Rubis-class SSN Saphir (S-602).

One of the greatest threats to a submarine on or near the surface comes from aircraft, whose approach is difficult for the submarine to detect under some circumstances. Some

Below: Mission sequence diagam of ship-attack Tomahawk missile. This system gives US submarines a long-range, anti-ship capability. The most significant problem is that of target acquisition and identification at long ranges and an external target designator maybe required in many circumstances. Note how Tomahawk is autonomously able to differentiate between friendly and hostile targets.

Tomahawk anti-ship version

Above: A Sub-Harpoon missile leaves the water powered by its rocket booster, after the sealing cap has been ejected and with the launch capsule hidden by the cloud of propellant smoke.

Below: Latest Soviet SLCM is the SS-NX-24 which is being tested by a specially-modified Yankee class former SSBN. Range of this large missile is estimated to be some 2,200nm.

Missile launch on approximate range and bearing

Ship detected and identified as friendly: search continued

Ship detected and identified as enemy: homing initiated

Search pattern

Tomahawk acquires target and attacks

years ago three IKL 540 submarines, a version of the German Type 206 built under licence by Vickers in the United Kingdom, were fitted for the submarine-launched anti-aircraft missile (SLAM) system. This was designed to mount a quadruple launcher for the Short Blowpipe short-range SAM in the fin and controlled from inside the submarine. There have been recent reports that the Soviet Navy has a similar system under development and other reports suggest that this has been installed in the sail of the Kilo-class SSKs. Such a system is more relevant to a diesel-electric submarine, with its need to approach the surface in order to run its diesels to recharge the batteries, than to a nuclear-powered submarine. No reports have been made of similar systems fitted to British or American boats but it would be an obvious move to make

Torpedoes

Since World War II vast sums have been expended on expensive and frequently abortive, torpedo programmes. The first generation of SSNs and SSBNs went to sea with torpedoes which had little better performance than those of World War II; indeed, in many cases, they dated back to that war. As recently as 1982, for example, the British SSN, HMS *Conqueror*, used two of the very elderly Mark 8 torpedoes to sink the Argentine cruiser ARA *General Belgrano* during the Falklands War.

Even today most torpedoes have top speeds little better (perhaps worse) than those of their quarry. The American Mark 46 torpedo, for example, has a speed of 40 knots which is just less than that of the Soviet Alfa and Akula classes, making a stern chase out of the question. Torpedoes have also been dogged by unreliability problems and reports from the South Atlantic conflict abound with stories of both the Royal Navy and the Argentine Navy suffering from malfunctioning torpedoes.

In general terms, the capabilities of torpedoes have tended to lag behind those of the sonars that acquire their targets; they are slow, lacking in range, noisy and, in many instances, unreliable as well. The USSR and some other nations are experimenting with electric motors; at the moment these produce torpedoes which are quiet, but slow and lacking in range. Improved performance in either can only be obtained by more battery power, which means bigger torpedoes, or a

Above: When everything works properly, the modern torpedo displays a fearsome destructive capability. This obsolete British frigate was hit by a Tigerfish torpedo launched from HMS Tireless *during a live firing trial. The warhead detonated beneath the centre of the target, breaking its back and causing it to quickly sink.*

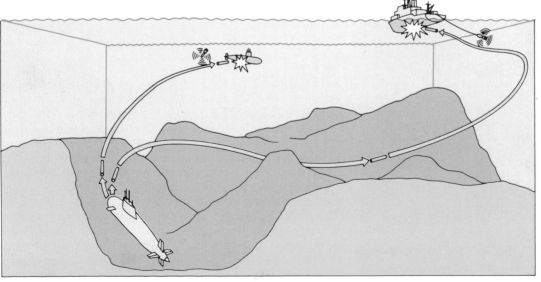

Right: Torpedoes are the essential submarine weapon system, designed to attack both surface and submerged targets. Surprisingly, torpedoes are also one of the most difficult areas of underwater technology.

Left: It is now feasible for attack submarines to carry out underwater ambushes, using the terrain of the seabed to mask their presence. Here, a submarine is shown attacking a surface warship, guiding its torpedo through underwater valleys to mask its approach, and, at the same time, it is attacking a hostile submarine. A further innovation is that on-board computers now enable torpedoes to avoid towed noise-makers (decoys).

smaller warhead, which could mean an ineffective torpedo. Torpedo sonar, too, needs to be improved and in America the Defense Advanced Projects Agency (DARPA) is working on this, possibly heading towards a torpedo with on-board signal processing, coupled with a two-way fibreoptic link to the parent submarine.

One answer to the lack of speed and range for torpedoes has been the development of a rocket-powered, airborne torpedo carrier. Launched from a standard torpedo tube, such weapons climb to the surface, travel through the air to the

Above: The periscope is one of the oldest and yet the most enduring of submarines' sensor systems. Here the captain of HMS Trafalgar views the scene on the ocean's surface.

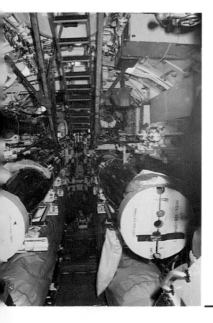

Submarine sensor and weapon systems

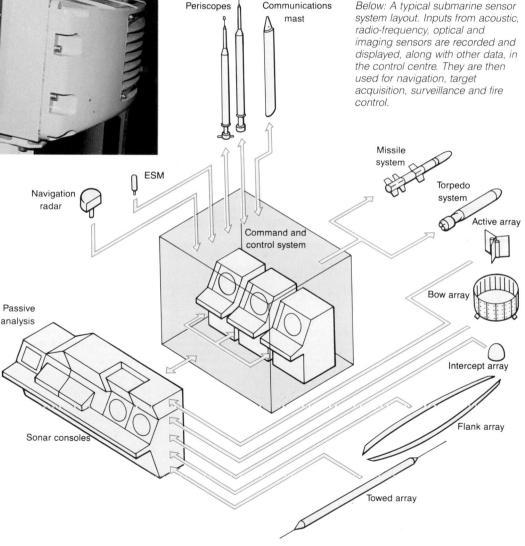

Below: A typical submarine sensor system layout. Inputs from acoustic, radio-frequency, optical and imaging sensors are recorded and displayed, along with other data, in the control centre. They are then used for navigation, target acquisition, surveillance and fire control.

Periscopes

Communications mast

Missile system

Torpedo system

Active array

Bow array

Intercept array

Flank array

Towed array

ESM

Navigation radar

Command and control system

Passive analysis

Sonar consoles

vicinity of the target and then drop the torpedo which seeks and destroys the target. Such systems include the American SUBROC (SUBmarine ROCket) and the Soviet SS-N-15, both 21in (533mm) weapons and the Soviet SS-N-16 which uses a 25.6in (65mm) tube. There is still, however, a need for a very much faster torpedo which does not leave the water. The American Advanced Capability (ADCAP) programme for the Mark 48 torpedo will raise the speed to 55 knots, while the British are developing the Spearfish, which uses a Sundstrand turbine and a pump-jet to attain a reported 76 knots.

Submarines in general are becoming very much larger, with some having double hulls, and are constructed of ever tougher materials, primarily in order to achieve greater diving depths. They are thus much stronger and more capable of surviving an attack. The problem of warhead effectiveness for torpedoes is serious and there is considerable current research to try to find a method of successfully penetrating the hulls of the newer submarines. Many torpedoes have shaped-charge warheads with a cone-shaped, copper-lined

Krupp MaK mine-laying system

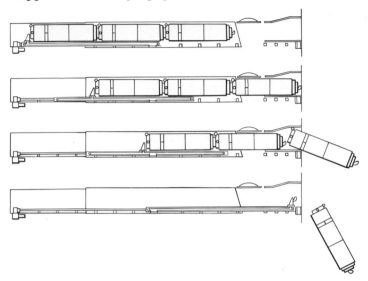

Below: The TR-1700 series of submarines is equipped with the new Krupp MaK hydraulic system for launching torpedoes. This technique uses hydraulic pressure rather than compressed air to eject the torpedo from the launch tube and is safer to use with the new types of torpedo propellants. The launching procedure utilises external water pressure, enabling torpedoes to be launched against the strong flow encountered when a submarine is travelling at high underwater speeds. The use of hydraulics also removes the problem of venting high-pressure compressed air into the submarine when launching a salvo of torpedoes in quick succession.

Above: Submarines are also extremely effective at covertly laying mines at choke points or along known submarine and shipping routes. Most launch mines through their torpedo tubes and this Krupp MaK system is typical of the methods used. A container holding three mines and an ejection system is inserted into the launch tube. In operation, a hydraulically operated piston rotates and pushes forward a continuous belt, which ejects each mine in turn. The forward part of the launch tube aligns the mine to the correct angle as it falls away to the sea bed. A submarine would normally carry two or three mine tubes in place of normal torpedoes or missiles.

Krupp MaK TR-1700 torpedo discharge system

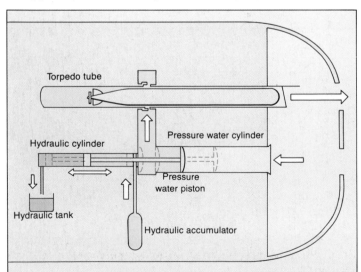

Torpedo tube

Hydraulic cylinder

Pressure water cylinder

Pressure water piston

Hydraulic tank

Hydraulic accumulator

recess at the front, which, when detonated, produces a narrowly focused explosive jet (the Monroe effect) with excellent penetration powers. The effect of such warheads is proportional to the diameter of the cone and thus one answer is simply to make larger diameter torpedoes. Many of the latest Soviet submarines now have at least two 25.6in (650mm) tubes for a new ASW torpedo with a speed of 45 knots over a range of 22nm (42km), using a wake-homing sensor. The only alternative is to use nuclear warheads. It is known that the Soviet Whiskey-class submarine that ran aground near the Swedish Karlskrona naval base in October 1981 carried nuclear-tipped torpedoes in its weapons load; estimated weapon yield is 15 kilotons.

Torpedo guidance systems vary considerably. The US Navy's Mark 46 torpedo, for example, has an active-passive homing head and either homes on the target's radiated noise or, if the target is silent, switches to active sonar. Another US Navy torpedo, the Mark 48 Mod 3, uses command guidance by wire in the mid-course part of its run, utilising a two-way link so that it can send sonar information back to the laun-

Below: For many years torpedoes followed a straight course after launch, which meant that if initial alignment was wrong, or the target took evasive action, they missed. Modern torpedoes, although still aimed at a target, have an autonomous search capability which enables them to carry out their own search pattern if no target is encountered. The Italian Whitehead A.244/S torpedo, for example, is launched when the firing vessel has manoeuvred into a position which gives the required hit probability. The torpedo travels on a pre-set bearing and depth with its acoustic homing head activated and searching for the target. After a straight run of predetermined length, if the torpedo has not acoustically acquired the target it initiates a curved search pattern which can be either a constant depth spiral (shown here), or a helix of varying depth and diameter. Modern homing torpedoes have the ability to recognise and identify target signatures from a pre-stored threat library and will ignore friendly vessels and acoustic decoys.

Whitehead A.244/S search pattern

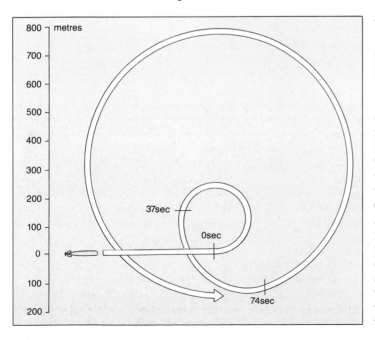

Above: The tactical plot on this British submarine is kept up to date by a rating with a grease pencil. Such manual methods are no longer capable of keeping up with the bewildering speed and *complexity of modern combat. Computerised electronic displays must be used to constantly collate and present information from on-board sensors, external sensors, other ships, aircraft and satellites.*

ching submarine; it then switches to an active-passive terminal homing head. The British Stingray guidance system is even more complex. On launch an active/passive sonar transducer works in the passive mode, but changes to the active mode automatically as soon as there is any indication that the target has become aware that it is under attack. Guidance wires link the torpedo to the launching submarine and, as with the American Mark 48 Mod 3, not only are commands fed to the torpedo but sonar data information is also passed back to the submarine's system. The wire is dispensed from both torpedo and submarine simultaneously, thus allowing the wire to remain stationary in the water. Essential as this is for the guidance system, it does, of course, have the effect of limiting the submarine's manoeuvres during the torpedo run.

Index